Practice for the New York State English Language Arts Assessment

Grade 4

Visit *The Learning Site!*
www.harcourtschool.com

Printed in the United States of America

ISBN 10: 0-15-374307-7
ISBN 13: 978-0-15-374307-8

2 3 4 5 6 7 8 9 10 018 16 15 14 13 12 11 10 09 08

Contents

Name ______________________________

UNIT 1 TEST

Reading

Directions

In this part of the test, you are going to do some reading. Then you will answer questions about what you have read.

Name ____

Directions

Read this story about Tony Beaver. Then answer questions 1 through 8.

Tony Beaver

At one time, the mountains of West Virginia were so rough and rocky that only the strongest and most determined pioneers could settle there. Even among those mighty pioneers, Tony Beaver was unusual.

By the time he was fifteen, Tony had to sit on the floor to eat at the table just to keep his head from bumping the ceiling. Tony could eat fifty pancakes and thirty eggs for breakfast. He would wash down the meal with ten gallons of milk. An entire carrot patch from the garden was his midmorning snack. Tree branches were his toothpicks.

At eighteen, Tony left home. He needed a job. He stepped from mountaintop to mountaintop. In his travels, Tony met Hannibal and Goliath, two very large oxen. Tony invited them to join him.

Before long, Tony and the oxen came to Turtle Cove. There Tony entered a wood-chopping contest. A lumberjack named Big Bill Simpson was running the contest. Big Bill explained that the person who could chop down the most trees in one hour would be the winner. The prize was a brand-new axe.

Tony had chopped down plenty of trees, so he sharpened his axe and took a few practice swings. Bill called, "Ready, set, go!" Tony swung his axe so hard that the huge hickory tree he was aiming at broke off like a matchstick. Hardly breaking a sweat, he chopped down seven trees for every tree most other contestants downed.

Tony was pleased to get the new axe. He was even happier when Big Bill hired him on the spot. That was the biggest reward of all. "You were born to be a lumberjack, son," Big Bill said. Big Bill was right about Tony Beaver's being a natural lumberjack. Before long, Tony could cut down one tree on a back swing and one on the down swing of the axe. After realizing there was a quicker way to get the job done, he started pulling trees out by the roots.

Because of his amazing strength and size, Tony Beaver became as big a celebrity in West Virginia as his cousin Paul Bunyan was up north. Tony Beaver gained fame as West Virginia's most powerful lumberjack.

> **TIP** Some words have multiple meanings. When you come to a multiple-meaning word such as *natural,* look at the words and sentences around it to help you figure out what it means in the story.

> **TIP** Paul Bunyan was a folktale lumberjack in the northern United States. Bunyan had a large ox named Blue.

Go On

Name ______________________________

1 According to the story, Tony Beaver left home to

A visit relatives
B find work
C go to school
D buy oxen

2 According to the story, why did Tony sit on the floor when he ate his meals?

F because the family didn't have enough chairs
G because the table was short
H to keep from hitting his head on the ceiling
J to eat in front of the warm fireplace

3 Big Bill said that Tony was born to be a lumberjack. The word "lumberjack" **most likely** means

A a tree cutter
B a mountain climber
C a farmer
D a rancher

4 Here is a web about Tony Beaver.

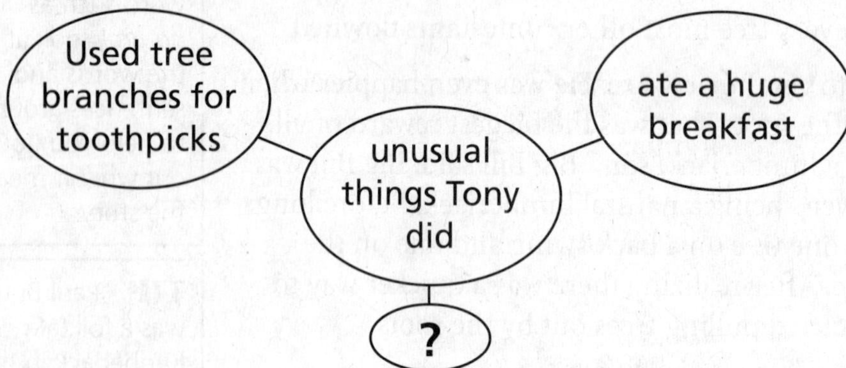

Which phrase **best** completes the web?

F chopped down a tree
G won an axe
H lived in West Virginia
J pulled trees out by the roots

Name ______________________________

5 Which sentence lets you know Tony won the contest?

A Hardly breaking a sweat, he chopped down seven trees for every tree most other contestants downed.

B Tony was pleased to get the new axe.

C He was even happier when Big Bill hired him on the spot.

D That was the biggest reward of all.

TIP Reread the contest rules and prizes and what happens at the end of the contest. Use the information to identify the sentence that makes it clear Tony won the contest.

6 Read these sentences from the story.

Big Bill was right about Tony Beaver's being a natural lumberjack.

The word "natural" **most likely** means

F found in nature

G having to do with nature and all the living things related to it

H what is usual in nature

J perfectly suited for because of ability present at birth

7 Which detail about Tony is **most** important to the story?

A Tony was big and strong.

B Tony won a contest.

C Tony was Paul Bunyan's cousin.

D Tony owned two huge oxen.

8 According to the story, why is Paul Bunyan mentioned?

F He lived in West Virginia.

G He was Tony's father.

H He was a huge, strong lumberjack like Tony.

J He won the wood-chopping contest.

Go On

Name ______________________________

Directions

Read this article about the Lewis and Clark Expedition. Then answer questions 9 through 15.

The Lewis and Clark Expedition

In 2004 the United States government issued nickels with new designs. These nickels celebrate the bicentennial of the Lewis and Clark Expedition. Two hundred years earlier, President Thomas Jefferson had sent explorers west. They were to explore new American lands.

In his first term as President, Jefferson nearly doubled the size of the United States in one move. He did this by buying a huge territory from the French government. This territory came to be called the Louisiana Purchase. The land stretched west from the Mississippi River to the Rocky Mountains.

President Jefferson asked his secretary, Meriwether Lewis, to head an expedition to find out more about the new land. Lewis asked Lieutenant William Clark to lead it with him.

The plan was to travel up the Missouri River, then walk to the Columbia River, and finally to travel by boat to the Pacific Ocean. Along the way, they would gather examples of plants and make notes about the animals. They would also make contact with the Native Americans who lived there.

In May of 1804, the expedition started. In the fall, the explorers arrived at a Mandan Indian village. There they hired a French trader to guide them through the unmapped region. The trader was accompanied by his Native American wife, Sacagawea. She proved to be a better guide and interpreter than her husband. She helped guide them through the unfamiliar territory.

After more than a year of exploring, the group reached the Continental Divide. This is the line at which the rivers start flowing west to the Pacific Ocean rather than east. They expected to find the Columbia River, but they could see only mountain after mountain stretching before them. Just when finding the river seemed hopeless, the explorers met a group of Shoshone Indians. Sacagawea recognized one of the chiefs as her own brother. He sold the group many horses and found them a guide.

Name ______________________________

More than two years after they began their journey, Lewis and Clark arrived back at their starting point in St. Louis, Missouri. People were afraid that everyone had died on the expedition, so the news of their arrival was a cause for celebration.

The Lewis and Clark Expedition was one of the most important journeys ever taken in this country. Not only did Lewis and Clark help map the territory, they also provided new information about the people, plants, and animals that lived there.

9 According to the article, a bicentennial is

A a big celebration
B a 200th anniversary
C an expedition
D a government coin

10 The Louisiana Purchase made the United States

F smaller
G part of France
H twice as large
J a territory

11 Which sentence tells what the article is **mostly** about?

A These nickels celebrate the bicentennial of the Lewis and Clark Expedition.
B In May of 1804, the expedition started.
C President Jefferson asked his secretary, Meriwether Lewis, to head an expedition to find out more about the new land.
D The Lewis and Clark Expedition was one of the most important journeys ever taken in this country.

TIP The main idea is the most important idea in a selection. Main ideas are often found at the beginning or end of an article. Look in these places for the main idea statement.

Go On

Name ______________________________

12 The chart below shows what happens in the article.

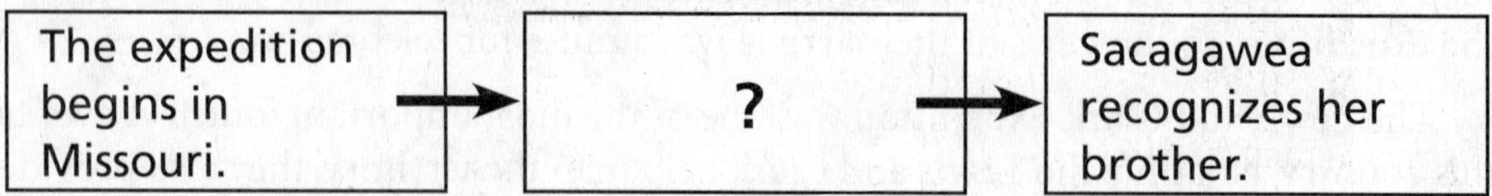
The expedition begins in Missouri.
?
Sacagawea recognizes her brother.

Which sentence **best** completes the chart?

F Jefferson makes the Louisiana Purchase.
G The expedition reaches the Continental Divide.
H Lewis and Clark arrive back at their starting point.
J The Shoshone chief sells them horses.

13 According to the article, why did Sacagawea join the expedition?

A She accompanied her husband.
B Lewis and Clark hired her.
C She wanted to visit her brother.
D She would make a good interpreter.

14 What did the explorers expect to find at the Continental Divide?

F the Columbia River
G the Missouri River
H the Pacific Ocean
J the Louisiana Purchase

15 According to the article, what was the **main** purpose of the expedition?

A to collect samples of minerals
B to make a map of the United States
C to keep records of the plants
D to find out more about the Louisiana Purchase

STOP

Name ______________________________

Listening and Writing

Directions

In this part of the test, you are going to listen to a story called "Flood." Then you will answer questions about the story.

You will listen to the story twice. The first time you hear the story, listen carefully but do not take notes. As you listen to the story the second time, you may want to take notes. Use the space below for your notes. You may use these notes to answer the questions that follow. Your notes on this page will NOT count toward your final score.

Notes

Do NOT turn this page until you are told to do so.

Name ______________________________

16 Tom's family reacts to the rising waters of the Mississippi River. In the boxes, record four events that take place after Pa tells the boys, "The river's rising."

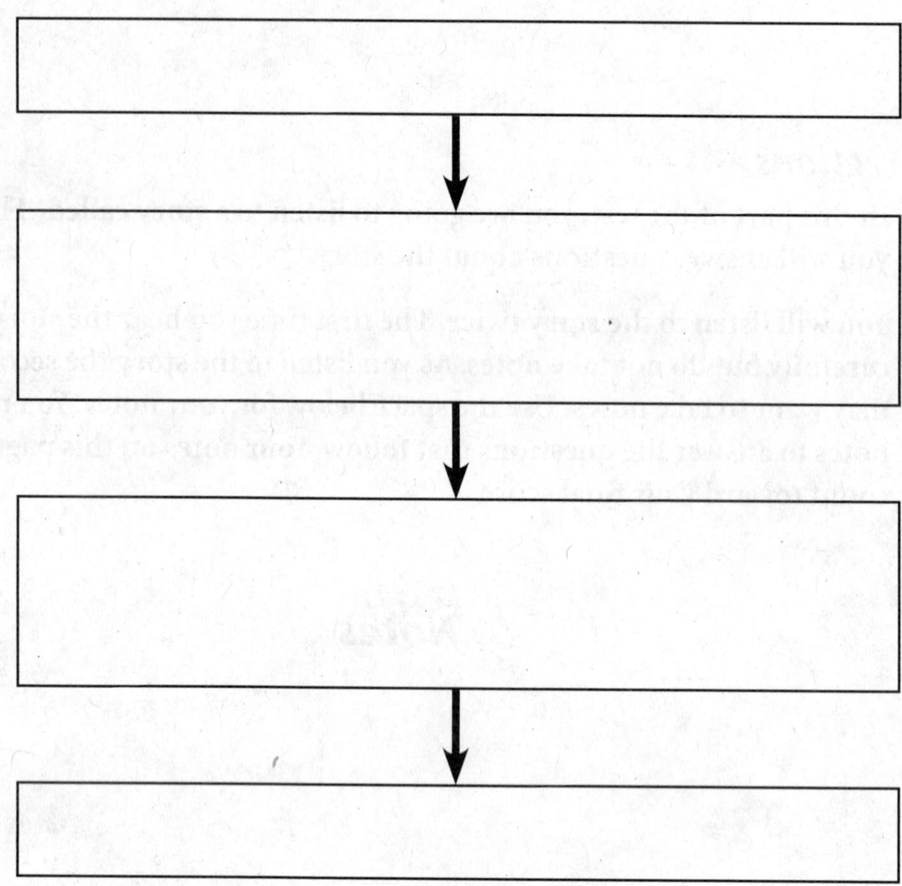

17 Explain why the family went to Baxter's Hill along with their animals. Use details from the story to support your answer.

____

____

____

Name ______________________________

Planning Page

You may PLAN your writing for question 18 here if you wish, but do NOT write your final answer on this page. Your writing on this Planning Page will NOT count toward your final score. Write your final answer beginning on the next page.

Name ______________________________

18

Write an ending to the story.
In your ending, be sure to tell
- how long the family stays on Baxter's Hill
- whether the family's farm is flooded
- what the family finds when they return to the farm
- what Tom and Billy do to help Pa
- if Tiny ever lays an egg

Check your writing for correct spelling, grammar, capitalization, and punctuation.

____

____

____

____

____

____

____

____

____

____

____

____

STOP

Name ______________________________

Reading and Writing

Directions

In this part of the test, you are going to read a story called "The Name of the Game" and an article called "Race for the Gold." You will answer questions 19 through 23 and write about what you have read. You may look back at the story and the article as often as you like.

Go On

Name ______________________________

The Name of the Game

Luis had been in Bay View City for only one week, and he missed his old home. It was hard enough leaving his friends and relatives, but leaving behind his country of Mexico was even harder.

The kids at his new school seemed friendly enough. They smiled at him, and they made room for him at the lunch table. None of them spoke Spanish, though, and Luis knew only a little English.

Every morning Luis went to a special classroom where a teacher taught him English. He was learning more and more, but it was still hard to talk with the other kids. He had to concentrate so much on the strange-sounding words that he sometimes got a headache. Luis missed being able to read and understand everything around him.

There were other things he missed, too. He missed the big midday meals with his family. In Mexico, everyone in the family would come home and eat a leisurely meal together. There would be a lot of talking and laughing, and no one seemed to be in a hurry.

Now his father ate lunch at work, and Luis ate lunch at school. Luis missed the tortillas, rice, and chicken his mother and grandmother used to prepare. Just thinking about it made his stomach growl. It was hard for him to get used to the food they served in the school cafeteria, and everyone had to eat so quickly.

Luis also missed his grandparents, aunts, uncles, and cousins. He wasn't used to the crowded sidewalks and the noisy traffic of the city. Most of all, he missed *fútbol.* That is the Spanish name for soccer.

In Mexico, Luis and his friends played *fútbol* whenever they weren't in school, eating, or sleeping. Sometimes older brothers, fathers, and uncles would join in the games. They would play in the evening until it got too dark to see the ball. No one seemed to play *fútbol* here in Bay View City.

Then one day at recess, one of the boys called, "Hey Luis! Do you want to play football with us?"

At last! Here was something familiar. Here was something he loved. Luis nodded excitedly and ran over to the group of kids.

"Maybe I can't understand everything they say," Luis thought, "but I understand *fútbol*!"

Name ______________________________

When the game began, though, it was not what he expected at all. This was American football. It was fun, but it was not the game Luis had played in Mexico.

"I don't think the kids here know how to play *fútbol,*" he told his family that night at dinner.

"Maybe you'll need to learn American football," his mother said.

Luis shrugged. "I guess so."

Every day at recess, Luis played American football. He became good at throwing and catching the ball. He liked the game well enough, but it still wasn't *fútbol.*

Then one Saturday afternoon, Luis got his old ball and took it down to the park. He was dribbling it across the grass when he heard someone call his name. Some boys from his class were waving at him.

"Hey, Luis! Can we play soccer with you?" one of them yelled.

Luis was confused. What was this *soccer* they were talking about?

"Come on, Luis! Kick the ball to me!" another boy called.

Luis grinned and kicked the ball. Before he knew it, he was in the middle of the game he loved best. When they finally stopped playing, the boys gathered around Luis.

"We didn't know you were such a great soccer player! Did you play soccer a lot in Mexico?"

So soccer is the English name for the game! Luis nodded. "In Mexico we call it *fútbol.*"

The boys laughed. "Well, let's play some more *fútbol*!" one of them said.

Luis grinned happily. Whether he called it soccer or *fútbol,* it was still his favorite game.

Go On

Name ____________________

19 Luis found that life in the United States was different from life in Mexico. Complete the chart to show differences.

	United States	Mexico
Language		
Midday meal		

20 Explain how Mexican fútbol, American football, and soccer are alike and different. Use details from the story to support your answer.

____

____

____

____

Name ______________________________

Race for the Gold

Wilma Rudolph was one of the greatest athletes of the twentieth century. At the 1960 Olympics in Rome, Rudolph broke an Olympic world record and also became the first American woman to win three gold medals in one Olympics.

A Challenging Childhood

Wilma Rudolph was born on June 23, 1940, in Clarksville, Tennessee. She was the twentieth child in a family of twenty-two children. Her father was a handyman and a railroad porter. Her mother cooked, cleaned, and did laundry for other families. Although they worked hard, the family was poor and they often struggled to make ends meet.

Wilma was a very small and sickly baby. She had many illnesses during the first few years of her life. When Wilma was four years old, she got polio, a dangerous disease that caused her to lose the use of her left leg. Doctors told her mother that Wilma would never be able to walk again.

Wilma's family did not let this news stop them. Undaunted, they began to work with Wilma. They were determined to bring her back to health. Twice a week for two years, Mrs. Rudolph took Wilma by bus to a special hospital. The doctors taught Wilma's mother how to do special exercises with Wilma at home.

Wilma's mother taught Wilma's brothers and sisters how to help with the exercises. Everyone in the family pitched in. They rubbed Wilma's legs four times a day. They encouraged her to believe she could get better. Soon Wilma could walk with a leg brace. By the time she was nine, she was walking normally. She decided to become an athlete.

Sprinting to Stardom

Wilma began playing basketball in high school. She was such a good player that she led her team to the state championship. She also started running track. When she was thirteen, Wilma ran and won twenty races. Her coach nicknamed her "Skeeter" because she always seemed to be buzzing around.

The track coach at Tennessee State University invited Wilma to a summer training camp. At the camp, Wilma ran twenty miles a day. At the end of the summer, Wilma went with the track team to a contest in Philadelphia. She won every race she entered.

Wilma was a junior in high school when she was chosen to join the Olympic track team. She was the youngest member on the team. Wilma helped the team win a bronze medal in the 1956 Olympics.

Go On

Name ___

After high school, Wilma entered Tennessee State University. She joined the women's track team. She attended the Olympic trials in 1960, and set a world record in the 200-meter race. No one would break her record for eight years!

Wilma was twenty when she competed at the 1960 Olympics in Rome. She took gold medals in the 100-meter and 200-meter races and won a third gold medal as one of the four members of the 400-meter relay team.

Wilma received many other awards for her great athletic ability. She was the first woman ever to receive some of these awards.

A True Champion

Wilma Rudolph never forgot that many people had helped her achieve success. She worked hard to give others the same advantages that she had been given. Rudolph coached young, poor athletes from around the country in a program called Operation Champion. She worked with several other community organizations as well.

Throughout her life, Wilma Rudolph helped prepare other African American female athletes for success. She coached runners at high schools and colleges around the country. She also created the Wilma Rudolph Foundation, a community-based sports program.

Rudolph wrote a book about her life, which was made into a movie. Both the book and the movie inspired other people to overcome their challenges as she had done.

Wilma Rudolph died in 1994. That same year, the governor of Tennessee made June 23 Wilma Rudolph Day in her home state.

Name ____________________

21 The chart below shows some of the events in Wilma's life. Complete the chart with another event from Wilma's life.

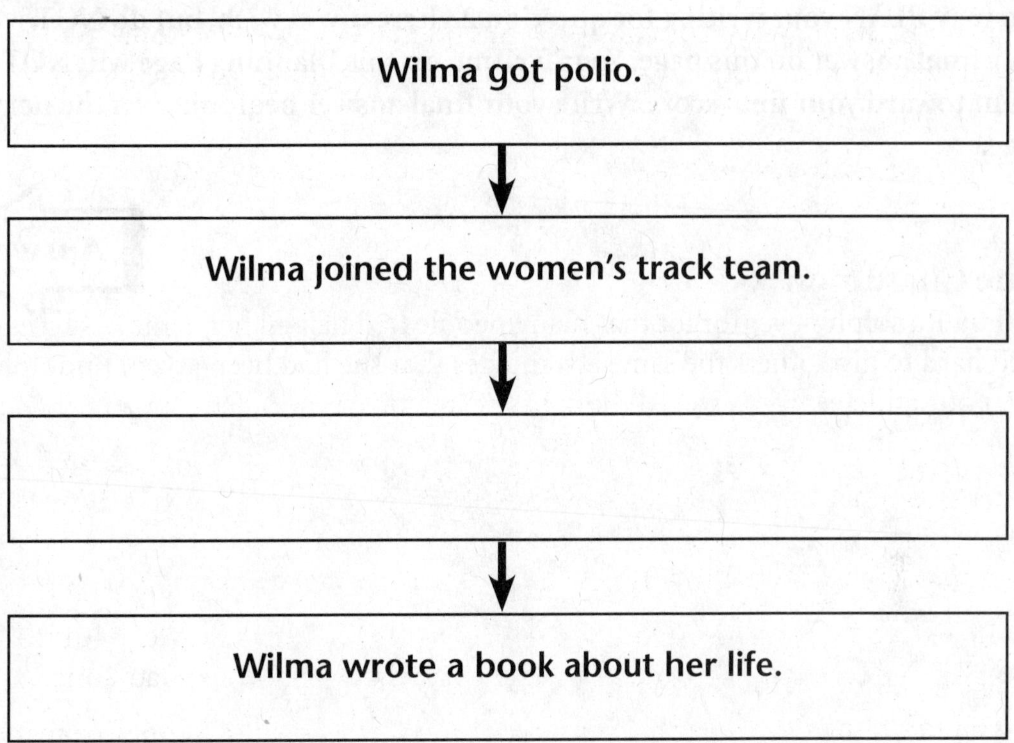

22 Explain how Wilma helped other athletes. Use details from the story to support your answer.

____

____

____

____

____

____

Go On

Name ______________________________

Planning Page

You may PLAN your writing for question 23 here if you wish, but do NOT write your final answer on this page. Your writing on this Planning Page will NOT count toward your final score. Write your final answer beginning on the next page.

Name ______________________________

23

Both Luis and Wilma had to overcome difficulties to succeed. Luis had to overcome cultural and social difficulties, and Wilma had to overcome physical problems. Suppose Luis and Wilma were being featured in a school newspaper article titled "People You Should Know." Write the article for the school paper.

In your article, be sure to tell

- what Luis's and Wilma's backgrounds are
- what problems they had to overcome and how they overcame them
- why they are people you should know
- how both used sports to help them overcome problems

Check your writing for correct spelling, grammar, capitalization, and punctuation.

____

____

____

____

____

____

____

____

____

____

____

Go On

Name

STOP

Name ______________________________

Revise and Edit Practice

Sample

There are some mistakes in this paragraph. Let's correct them together.

i live in a small town. I knows most of the people who live here. My friend and I walk to School each day. It takes about 10 minutes to walk to school. The school is two blocks from our houses?

Go On

Name ____

Here is a paragraph a student wrote. There are some mistakes in the paragraph. Some sentences may have more than one mistake, and other sentences may contain no mistakes at all. There are no mistakes in spelling.

Read the paragraph, and find the mistakes. Draw a line through each mistake in the paragraph. Then write the correction above it.

our mall is at the end of Michigan street. My mother and I go to the mall to shop and eat lunch. The mall are huge! It have an ice skating rink in the middle. the building has three levels. The stores are located according to what they sell. for example, the entire second floor has nothing but shoe stores.

STOP

Name ___

UNIT 2 TEST

Reading

Directions

In this part of the test, you are going to do some reading. Then you will answer questions about what you have read.

Name ______________________________

*D*irections

Read this story about a frog named Wishing Well. Then answer questions 1 through 6.

Wishing Well Gets His Wish

"Look, Mom!" said Lianne. "I won this frog at Irene's backyard carnival. Isn't he cute? I'm going to name him Wishing Well because I won him in the Wishing Well contest."

While Lianne was talking to her mother, she put some water in the container and closed it up again. Wishing Well bumped against the top of the container as he hopped.

"Do you think the frog will like being in that container?" asked Lianne's mother.

"Sure. It has water inside and holes in the top for air. I would like it if I were a frog," Lianne said.

"Really? Would you like it if someone put you in a tiny room with no toys, no friends, and nothing fun to do? You would have to eat whatever someone dropped in, even if it was brussels sprouts."

"I don't like brussels sprouts much," said Lianne.

"Well, you'd have to eat them if that was all you had. Think about it, Lianne."

With a sigh, Lianne looked at Wishing Well bumping woefully around the plastic container. He was such a beautiful frog. It would be so nice to have him as a pet.

However, the pond was Wishing Well's true home. Lianne thought quietly for a minute. She could imagine Wishing Well swimming deep under lily pads and then popping up with only his eyes showing.

She picked up the plastic container. "Want to take a walk to the pond with me, Mom?" she asked with a little smile.

Name ______________________________

1 This story is **mostly** about

A Wishing Well
B Lianne
C Lianne's mother
D Irene

2 According to the passage, what is Wishing Well's **main** problem?

F The container is not tall enough to jump in.
G He likes the container.
H He is swimming under a lily pad.
J There isn't enough air in the container.

3 According to the passage, what is Lianne's **most important** character trait?

A She cares about animals.
B She likes to win contests.
C She always listens to her mother.
D She does not like brussels sprouts.

4 According to the passage, the word "woefully" **most likely** means

F without stopping
G doing the same things over and over again
H in a way that is full of sadness
J as a result of not being strong

Go On

Name ______________________________

5 Which of these would be another good title for the passage?

A "The Backyard Carnival"
B "Eating Brussels Sprouts"
C "A Difficult Decision"
D "Frogs Are Fun"

6 This is a chart of Lianne's activities.

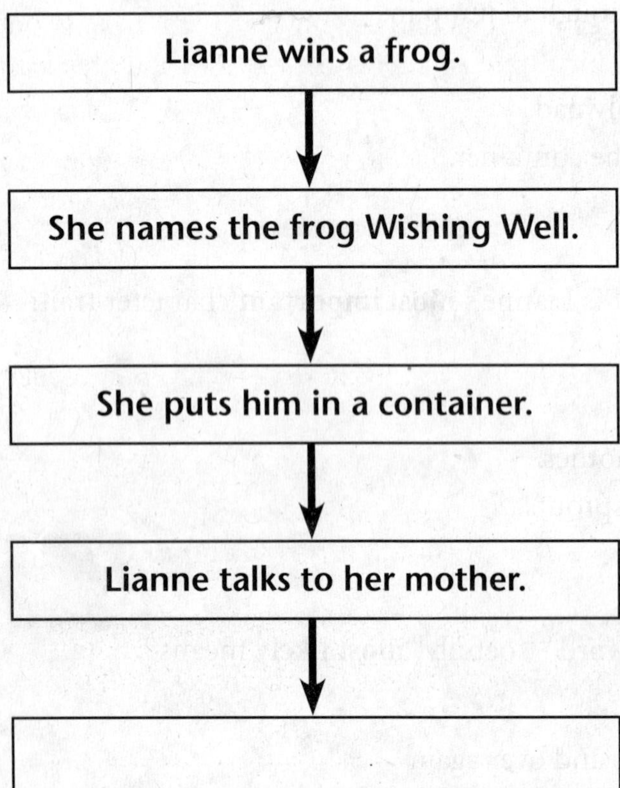

Which sentence **best** completes the chart?

F Lianne's mother gives her permission to keep the frog.
G Lianne and her mother go shopping.
H Lianne and her mother go for a swim.
J Lianne and her mother set the frog free.

Name ______________________

*D*irections

Read this article about manatees. Then answer questions 7 through 14.

Gentle Giants

Manatees are giant mammals that live in warm, shallow ocean waters and rivers near the coast. They are harmless animals that feed on huge amounts of sea grass, water lettuce, and other plants. A full-grown manatee can eat 100 to 150 pounds of plants a day!

Florida is home to the world's largest manatee population—about 2,400 manatees. The population grows slowly because female manatees usually give birth to only one infant every two to five years. The low birth rate is one reason why the manatee is in danger of disappearing forever.

Humans and their speedboats are especially dangerous for manatees. Manatees are slow swimmers that swim close to the water's surface. The propeller blades of a fast-moving motorboat can strike a manatee and cause serious injury.

There are ways to help keep manatees safe. Because the drivers of fast-moving boats can't see manatees underwater until it is too late, experts support slow-speed zones for boaters in areas where manatees live. Another idea is to have boaters place propeller guards on their boats.

One way to help manatees is to protect their homes by keeping waters clean and limiting building on nearby land. Protecting manatees in these ways may help to make sure these interesting and gentle creatures will be around for a long time.

weight at birth	60–70 pounds
adult weight	1,500–1,800 pounds
food per day	100–150 pounds of plants
life span	60 years
average swimming speed	3–5 miles per hour
top swimming speed	20 miles per hour

Go On

Name ______________________________

7 This article gives information about manatees by using

- **A** pictures and drawings
- **B** questions and answers
- **C** a true story about a rescued manatee
- **D** text and a chart

8 How can you find out the rate that manatees swim in miles per hour?

- **F** by skimming the article
- **G** by reading the text
- **H** by looking at the chart
- **J** by using both the text and the chart

9 What information about manatees is found in **both** the chart and the text?

- **A** the amount of food eaten per day
- **B** the weight of a full-grown adult
- **C** the birth rate of manatees
- **D** how many manatees there are in Florida

10 According to the article, what is one way to protect manatees?

- **F** Move the manatees to rivers with fewer boats.
- **G** Teach manatees to swim faster.
- **H** Build special cages for the manatees to live in.
- **J** Protect manatees' homes by limiting building on nearby land.

Name ______________________________

11 If humans don't take action to protect manatees,

A the manatees' food supply could run out
B boaters will need propeller guards
C manatees could disappear
D manatees will leave Florida for new homes in other places

12 According to the article, which of the following is **true** about manatees?

F They have short life spans.
G They try to hide from speedboats.
H They eat a lot.
J They like to jump and dive.

13 According to the article, you can tell that the author

A cares about manatees
B thinks people should not own boats
C wants readers to visit Florida
D has a boat with a propeller guard

14 Which of these sentences should be included in a summary of this article?

F Baby manatees weigh 60 to 70 pounds at birth.
G I think we need new laws to keep manatees safe.
H Some people use propeller guards on their boats.
J Humans cause the greatest danger to manatees.

STOP

Name ________________________________

Listening and Writing

Directions

In this part of the test, you are going to listen to a story called "The Travelers and the Bear." Then you will answer some questions about the story.

You will listen to the story twice. The first time you hear the story, listen carefully but do not take notes. As you listen to the story the second time, you may want to take notes. Use the space below. You may use these notes to answer the questions that follow. Your notes on this page will NOT count toward your final score.

Notes

Do NOT turn this page until you are told to do so.

Name ____

15 In "The Travelers and the Bear," Kan learns something about his friend Richard while they are hiking in the mountains. In the boxes below, explain what Kan decides and what causes his decision.

How does Richard's decision affect Kan's decision?

↓

What does Kan decide?

Go On

Name ______________________________

Planning Page

You may PLAN your writing for question 16 here if you wish, but do NOT write your final answer on this page. Your writing on this Planning Page will NOT count toward your final score. Write your final answer on the next page.

Name

16 Some stories try to teach us a lesson or moral. What is the moral of this story? Do you agree with it? How could it apply to your life?

Check your writing for correct spelling, grammar, capitalization, and punctuation.

STOP

Name ______________________________

Reading and Writing

Directions

In this part of the test, you are going to read a story called "Smokey" and an article called "How to Listen to a Pet." You will answer questions 17 through 19 and write about what you have read. You may look back at the story and the article as often as you like.

Name ______________________________

Smokey

Jenna watched the mail truck wind its way up Hawk Hill. By the time it finally pulled into the front yard, her mother had joined her on the porch.

"Morning, folks," Tina Martinez said, climbing out of the truck with a stack of mail.

"Good morning, Tina," said Jenna's mother. "Would you like a cup of coffee before you go?"

Tina smiled. "I'd like to, but I can't. Everyone on this hill has mail today. I'll be lucky to get home by dark. Thanks anyway." She smiled at Jenna as she handed Jenna's mother the mail. "How's Smokey, Jenna?"

"He's fine, thank you," replied Jenna.

Tina got back into the truck. She waved as she drove off. "See you later!" she called.

"Is any of that mail for me, Mom?"

Jenna's mother shook her head. "Sorry, no."

Jenna sighed. She wished some of her old friends would write to her. Ever since her family had moved to the country, she'd been lonely. There was no one her age for miles, and school wouldn't start for another month. The only companion she had was her cat, Smokey. She'd had him since he was a tiny kitten, and she couldn't imagine being without him. Smokey loved exploring, and he sometimes found the funniest places to sleep. Once Jenna had found him asleep in her sock drawer.

"Here, Smokey," she called. Playing with her cat always made Jenna feel less lonely. She called again, but Smokey did not come. Smokey was nowhere to be found.

"Mom, have you seen Smokey?"

Jenna's mother looked up from her computer. "Not since breakfast. Maybe he's hunting mice in the meadow."

Jenna went outside and walked to the meadow. She called Smokey's name as she made her way through the tall grass, but there was no sign of him. Jenna started to worry. What if he had wandered down to the road? What if he was lost in the woods behind the house?

Jenna searched for Smokey on and off throughout the day, with no luck. When she heard her father's truck that evening, she ran out to meet him.

"Dad, you didn't see Smokey on your way here, did you?" Jenna asked anxiously.

"No. Is he missing?"

"Since this morning," Jenna said with a lump in her throat. "What if he's hurt?"

Jenna's father ruffled her hair. "Oh, I'm sure he'll show up for dinner."

Go On

Name ______________________________

But Smokey didn't show up. After she had eaten, Jenna went out on the front porch to watch for him until it was too dark to see. Jenna was really worried now. "Smokey has never been gone this long before," she thought.

Just then Jenna saw two tiny headlights far off in the darkness. As she watched, they came steadily closer. Who could be visiting at this hour? No one ever came up Hawk Hill at night.

"Mom! Dad! Someone's coming!" Jenna called. Her parents came out and watched with her. When the mail truck stopped in front of the house, the three of them stared in surprise.

"Tina!" said Dad. "What are you doing here at this time of night?"

"I've got a special delivery for Jenna," Tina said.

"For me?" Jenna ran to the truck. "What is it?"

Tina pointed to a large, open mail sack. When Jenna peered inside, she saw two green eyes looking up at her.

"Smokey!" Jenna lifted up her cat and held him close. "Where did you find him?"

"Right there," Tina answered. "By the time I noticed him, I had finished my rounds. I'm sorry it took me so long."

"Oh, thank you, thank you!" Jenna cried happily. Smokey purred under her chin.

"How about that cup of coffee now, Tina?" Jenna's mother asked with a smile.

Name ______________________________

17 Using details from the story, complete the chart below. Think about the sequence of events that take place at the beginning, middle, and ending of the story. Write what happens in the correct order.

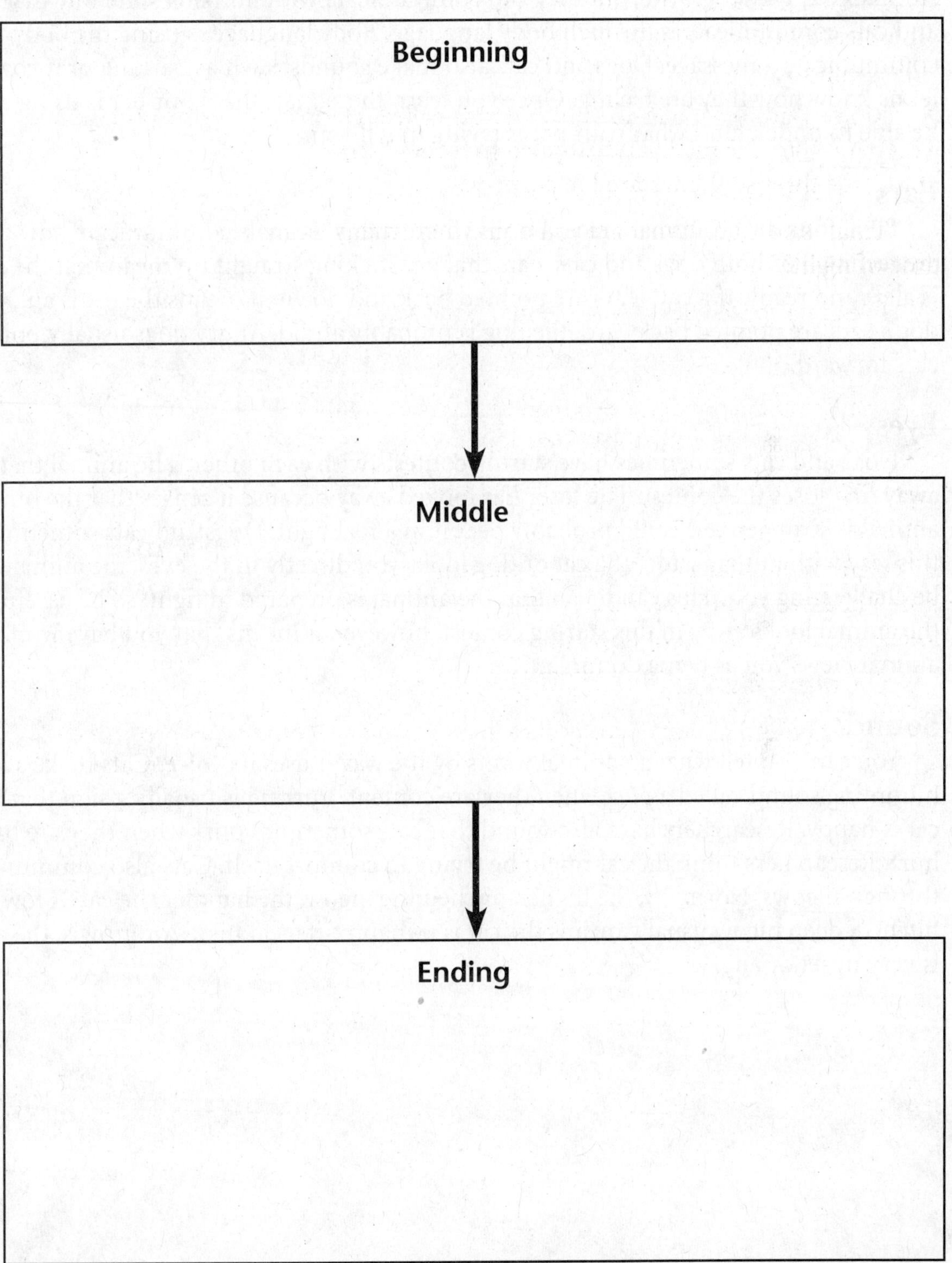

Go On

Name ___

How to Listen to a Pet

Human beings communicate in many ways. We can talk, write, and use sign language. Animals can't talk or write, but they can communicate with humans. One way that dogs and cats communicate is through body language. Body language is using the body to communicate a message. Dogs and cats also make sounds, such as barking or meowing, to let us know how they are feeling. Once you learn the signals that your pet is using, you'll be able to understand what your pet is trying to tell you.

Ears

First, look at the animal's face. This is where many animals communicate how they are feeling. For both dogs and cats, ears that are sticking straight up mean that the animal is alert and ready. If a cat's ears are pointed back and down, it means the cat is angry. If a dog's ears are pointed backward, the dog is probably afraid. Angry dogs usually point their ears forward.

Eyes

Dogs and cats sometimes have staring contests with each other. The animal that looks away first loses the contest. The loser has looked away because it senses that the other animal is stronger and could probably beat it in a real fight. Dogs and cats sometimes act this way with humans, too. If a cat or dog looks you directly in the eyes, the animal may be challenging you. This can mean that the animal is prepared to fight, so be careful. If the animal looks away in this staring contest, however, it means that you have won. The animal views you as being dominant.

Sounds

You can also tell what an animal wants by the way it uses its voice. Cats make a low humming sound called a *purr* when they are content. Purring is usually a sign that a cat is happy. Researchers have also found that cats sometimes purr when they are badly hurt. Researchers think the cat might be trying to comfort itself. Cats also communicate through meows. Normally, the higher-pitched the meow, the happier the cat. A low-pitched, deep meow usually means the cat is unhappy. If a cat hisses or growls, the animal is very upset or angry.

Name ______________________________

Dogs also use their voices to communicate with humans. The most common sound a dog makes is a bark. Quick, short barks usually mean that the dog is excited about something. The bark that dogs use most often is a loud, noisy bark. This means that something strange is happening and the dog is aware of it. The strange event could be a new person entering the room or the sound of another dog barking. When a dog is afraid, it might whimper. Like a cat, a dog will growl when angry.

Tails

What a dog or cat does with its tail can tell you a lot about how it is feeling. If a cat is scared, it will tuck its tail between its legs. If a cat is happy, its tail will stick straight up. When a cat swishes its tail back and forth, the cat is trying to say, "I am annoyed." If a dog wags its tail in the same way, however, you should interpret it as "I'm happy and ready to play." Dogs, like cats, tuck their tails between their legs when they are frightened. A dog will normally point its tail straight out if it is angry or looking for a fight.

Humans may never be able to know exactly what animals are thinking, but being able to interpret their signs and signals can help. Picking up the signals your pet sends can help you understand its mood, its wants, and its needs.

18 There are different sounds described in "How to Listen to a Pet." Give one cat sound and one dog sound, and tell what each means. Use details from the article to support your answer.

1. cat sound

____

____

2. dog sound

____

____

Go On

Name ______________________________

Planning Page

You may PLAN your writing for question 19 here if you wish, but do NOT write your final answer on this page. Your writing on this Planning Page will NOT count toward your final score. Write your final answer beginning on the next page.

Answer

Name ______________________________

19

Write a creative story about a cat or dog that uses body language to communicate with a person. Use what you read in "Smokey" and "How to Listen to a Pet."

In your story, be sure to include
- a title for your story
- a clear beginning, middle, and ending to your story
- specific details about animals and how they communicate

Check your writing for correct spelling, grammar, capitalization, and punctuation.

Go On

Name ____________________

STOP

Name ______________________________

Revise and Edit Practice

Sample

There are some mistakes in this paragraph. Let's correct them together.

Have you ever visited New york City? My class went to see the statue of Liberty. we also went to see a play on Broadway. I had took this same trip last winter. Before it snowed.

Go On

Name ______________________________

Here is a paragraph a student wrote. There are some mistakes in the paragraph. Some sentences may have more than one mistake, and other sentences may contain no mistakes at all. There are <u>no</u> mistakes in spelling.

Read the paragraph and find the mistakes. Draw a line through each mistake in the paragraph. Then write the correction above it.

There are many things to see when you visit a art museum. Do you have a favorite artist. My favorite artist is mary Cassatt. Her paintings is easy to understand. You don't have to guess about what's in the painting. choose an artist you admire and learn more about that artist.

STOP

Name ______________________________

UNIT 3 TEST

Reading

Directions

In this part of the test, you are going to do some reading. Then you will answer questions about what you have read.

Name ______________________________

Directions

Read this story about prairie grass. Then answer questions 1 through 8.

Growing a Patch of the Prairie

Kim was walking to the library when she saw her neighbor, Margo, in her yard. Margo was writing "For Sale" on a big piece of cardboard. On the sidewalk beside her were a lawn mower, two sprinklers, and four garden hoses.

TIP The "For Sale" sign is probably a clue about something that happens in the story. Why do you think someone would sell a lawn mower?

"Hi, Margo," said Kim. "It looks like you're having a sale."

"Yes, indeed," said Margo happily. "I'm selling my lawn."

Kim was a little puzzled. "How can you sell your lawn?" she asked.

"Well, I'm not really selling the lawn," said Margo. "I'm just getting a new kind of grass."

Margo's lawn was the prettiest in the neighborhood. Kim often saw Margo working in her yard.

"But your grass is perfect!" exclaimed Kim.

"I know. It's perfectly green because I feed it and water it so much. I've decided that it's perfectly wrong for this area. Today, people are bringing me my new buffalo grass."

Kim thought about grass that buffaloes would eat. She imagined a little piece of the Great Plains in Margo's yard. "Are you planting a prairie?" she asked.

"Exactly!" exclaimed Margo. "This is the same grass that settlers used to build sod houses. Buffalo grass can grow without having much extra water. Since it grows only eight inches tall, I'll mow it only a couple of times a year. I'm going to get a mower that I can power myself. Without the loud engine running, I can hear the birds while I cut the grass."

TIP Try to imagine what a prairie looks like. How do you think it is different from a regular lawn?

"If you're not taking care of your grass, when will I see you?" Kim asked.

Margo laughed. She seemed pleased by Kim's question. "Do you see those two chairs on the porch? Those chairs are for us to sit in while we look at the buffalo grass. We can relax and admire the grass from the porch. I'll have more time for relaxing than I ever had before."

Name ______________________________

1 This story **mostly** takes place

A at the library
B in Kim's yard
C on a prairie
D in Margo's yard

TIP Most of these places are mentioned in the passage, but only one tells where the story happens.

2 According to the story, Margo is selling

F her lawn mower, sprinklers, and hoses
G her yard
H a big piece of cardboard
J two chairs on her porch

TIP Which answer makes sense in the story? Cross out the answers that do not make sense.

3 Which statement about the story is a **fact**?

A Margo spends too much time in her yard.
B Margo's grass is the prettiest in the neighborhood.
C Kim often sees Margo working in her yard.
D Everyone should grow buffalo grass.

4 Which of the following would **best** fill in the box of this cause-and-effect chart?

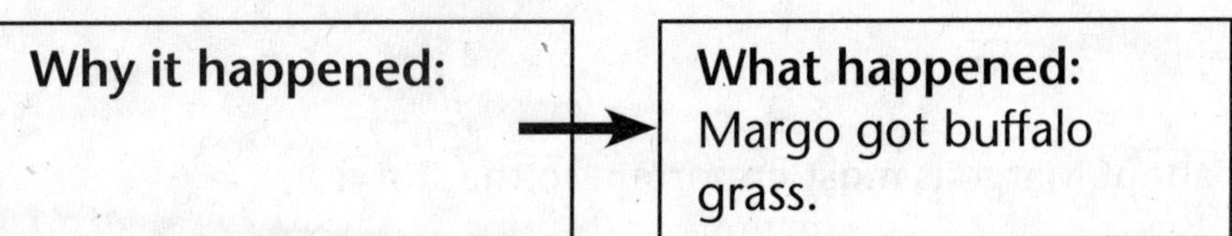

Why it happened:
What happened:
Margo got buffalo grass.

F Margo likes buffaloes.
G Margo's lawn is wrong for the area.
H Margo wants to take a vacation.
J Margo likes lawn mowers.

Go On

Name ______________________________

5 Read this sentence from the story.

We can relax and admire the grass from the porch.

The word "admire" means about the same as

- **A** regret getting
- **B** touch
- **C** take care of
- **D** look fondly at

6 Why did the writer **most likely** write this passage?

- **F** to describe the best way to water a lawn
- **G** to urge people to mow their lawns more often
- **H** to tell people about a kind of grass that saves time and water
- **J** to persuade people to buy lawnmowers

7 According to the story, what will **most likely** happen next?

- **A** Margo will go to the library with Kim.
- **B** Margo will water her lawn more.
- **C** Margo will plant a vegetable garden.
- **D** Margo will spend more time relaxing on her porch.

TIP The story doesn't tell what will happen next. You need to draw a conclusion by using clues from the story.

8 Which detail about Margo is **most** important to the story?

- **F** She knows about sod houses.
- **G** She likes when Kim visits.
- **H** She likes to work in her yard.
- **J** She is getting a new lawn.

Name ______________________________

Directions

Read this passage about prairie dogs. Then answer questions 9 through 16.

Visiting a Prairie Dog Town

If you were out on the prairie, you might notice something strange. First, you might see an area filled with small, round holes. Then, you might see a few heads or even entire bodies of small animals peeking out from those holes. As you moved closer, you would hear some high-pitched noises, and suddenly all the animals would disappear into their holes. Finally, you would know you were looking at a prairie dog town.

TIP As you read, ask questions that will help you understand the passage. For example, why would you find small, round holes in a prairie? Read on to find the answer.

Prairie dogs, however, are not really dogs. They are called "dogs" because they make a barking sound, especially when they sense danger nearby. Prairie dogs are actually members of the squirrel family.

Prairie dogs live in burrows, which are underground tunnels that connect to one another. These connected tunnels can spread out for acres. Inside their burrows, the prairie dogs live in family groups. These family groups warn each other about danger. Prairie dogs help keep one another clean, and they play together, too.

TIP If you are not familiar with a word in the passage, don't let that confuse you. Read on to learn more about it. The word will often be explained in the passage.

Prairie dogs can help keep up the land because they often eat grasshoppers and other insects. Unfortunately, some prairie dogs are killed by people who want to use the land for other things. If people are not careful, prairie dog towns could turn into ghost towns.

Go On

Name ___

9 According to the passage, prairie dogs are members of which animal family?

A cat
B mole
C dog
D squirrel

10 According to the passage, why are prairie dogs called "dogs"?

F They make good pets.
G They bark.
H They wag their tails.
J They look like dogs.

11 What is something that prairie dogs do to help keep up the land?

A clean each other
B play together
C eat grasshoppers
D warn each other of danger

12 Here is a web about prairie dogs.

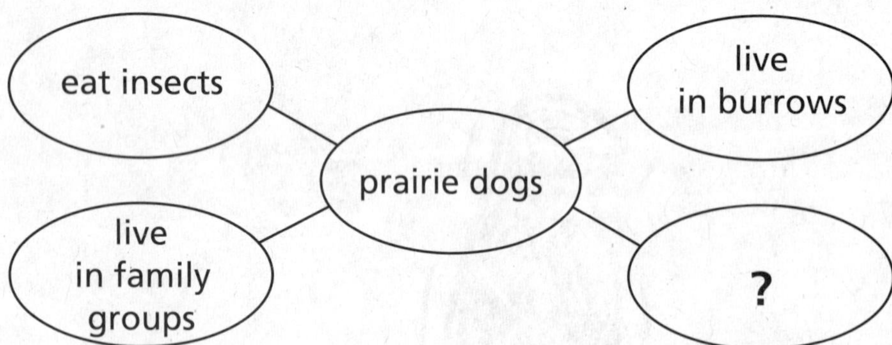

Which phrase **best** completes the web?

F look like large dogs
G bark like dogs
H warn people about danger
J make good pets

Name ______________________________

13 According to the passage, the word "burrows" means

A prairie dogs
B squirrels
C underground tunnels
D neighborhoods

14 You can look for prairie dogs by

F looking for round holes in a prairie
G looking for squirrels
H listening for danger
J looking in trees

15 According to the passage, some prairie dogs are killed

A because other animals eat them
B because people want to use the land
C because there is no food for them to eat
D because they get too close to busy streets

16 The author **most likely** wrote this article to

F give readers information about prairie dogs
G explain why prairie dogs bark
H describe what life was like on a prairie
J tell readers a funny story about the prairie

STOP

Name ______________________________

Listening and Writing

Directions

In this part of the test, you will listen to a story called "The Mystery Maps." Then you will answer questions about the story.

You will listen to the story twice. The first time you hear the story, listen carefully but do not take notes. As you listen to the story the second time, you may want to take notes. Use the space provided below. You may use these notes to answer the questions that follow. Your notes on this page will NOT count toward your final score.

Notes

Do NOT turn this page until you are told to do so.

Name ____

17 In "The Mystery Maps," Annika leads Martine, Natasha, and Valerie on a treasure hunt with a map. Retrace the sequence of events to explain what happens in the story.

1.

↓

2.

↓

3.

↓

4.

↓

5.

Go On

Name ______________________________

Planning Page

You may PLAN your writing for question 18 here if you wish, but do NOT write your final answer on this page. Your writing on this Planning Page will NOT count toward your final score. Write your final answer beginning on the next page.

Name ______________________________

18 In "The Mystery Maps," Annika found a creative way to invite guests to a party. Pretend you are throwing a party. Write a traditional party invitation in the form of a letter. Be sure to include where and when the event will take place, a description of the event, and directions on how to get to the event from your school.

Check your writing for correct spelling, grammar, capitalization, and punctuation.

STOP

Name ______________________________

Reading and Writing

Directions

In this part of the test, you are going to read a story called "New Friends" and an article called "A Trip Through Ellis Island." You will answer questions 19 through 21 and write about what you have read. You may look back at the story and the article as often as you like.

Name ______________________________

New Friends

Helen Sims was feeling proud. Her class was starting a pen pal project, and it had been her idea. Last summer at soccer camp, Helen became friends with a girl named Fernanda who lived in Brazil. Helen and Fernanda agreed to write each other at least once a month.

Helen told Mrs. Parker, her teacher, about her new pen pal. Mrs. Parker became excited.

"We're going to be studying South America," Mrs. Parker said to Helen. "It would be great for our class to communicate with some students in Brazil. Could you ask your friend to send me the name and address of her teacher? I'll write and ask if our two classes can become pen pals."

"I'll e-mail her tonight," said Helen.

A week later, Mrs. Parker announced the plan to the students. "Each class will send and receive a letter a month."

"Can we ask them questions?" asked Daniel. "I want to find out if they have been to a rain forest."

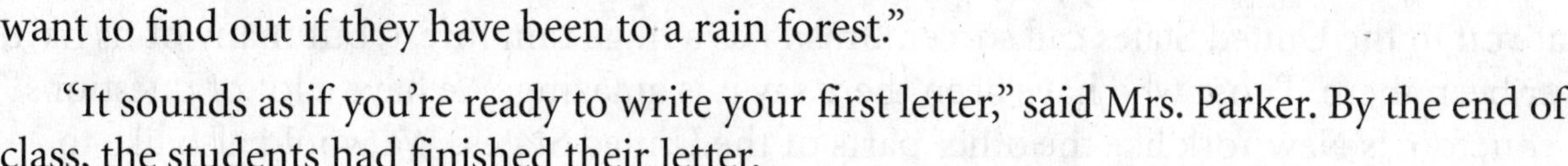

"It sounds as if you're ready to write your first letter," said Mrs. Parker. By the end of class, the students had finished their letter.

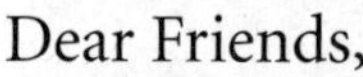

Dear Friends,

Greetings from the United States! We are glad to be pen pals with you. We live in the state of New York. It is in the eastern part of the country on the Atlantic Ocean. We live in New York City, the city with the largest population in the United States. More than 8 million people live here!

We can't wait to find out about Brazil. What language do you speak? Do any of you besides Fernanda speak English? What are your favorite sports? What kind of music do you listen to? We know that the Amazon rain forest is in Brazil. Have any of you ever been to a rain forest? What is it like? What is your city like? Write back soon!

Sincerely,
Mrs. Parker's Class
Lincoln Park Elementary School
New York, New York
United States of America

Go On

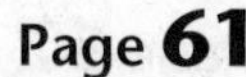

Name ______________________________

Two weeks passed. No letter came from Brazil. More time passed. Finally, Tamika said, "I don't think this is working. By the time we get their first letter, we might be finished studying South America."

"It is taking longer than I expected," admitted Mrs. Parker. "Does anyone have any ideas?"

"We could have an express delivery company deliver our letter," suggested Paul.

"That should get it there fast, but it would cost a lot of money," Daniel said.

"I have an idea," said Helen. "I will e-mail the letter to Fernanda, and she can print it and take it to her class. Then she can e-mail her class's letter back to me."

"Great idea," said Helen's friend Dory. The rest of the class agreed.

That night Helen sent the class' letter to Fernanda. Two days later, she got back this letter by e-mail:

Dear Mrs. Parker's Class,

Olá from Brasil! We enjoyed reading your letter. Our city, São Paulo, is the largest in Brasil. In fact, it is the largest city in South America. More than 10 million people live here. Most people in Brasil speak Portuguese. Our class has learned some English as well.

We enjoy many different sports in Brasil, but *futebol* is the most popular. *Futebol* is what you in the United States call soccer. Brasil has a huge rain forest, but many of us have never been there. Those who have been there say it is amazing. We have a lot of questions for you, too. Is New York like the other parts of the United States? We would also like to know more about you. What are your favorite sports? What do you like to eat?

Your idea to send letters by e-mail is a really good one. We can even send photos to each other!

Sincerely,
Your friends in Senhora Branco's Class
São Paulo, Brasil

"What a great letter," Helen said to herself. "The class will love it!"

Go On

Name ______________________________

19 Mrs. Parker's class learned about life in Brazil from their pen pals in Senhora Branco's class. Use details from the passage and what you already know to compare life in the United States with life in Brazil.

	United States	Brazil
Largest Cities		
Languages		
Favorite Sports		
Geography		

Go On

Name ______________________________

A Trip Through Ellis Island

Ellis Island was an immigration station in New York Harbor. Many people who were moving to the United States from other countries had to pass through Ellis Island. Between 1892 and 1954, about 12 million immigrants entered the United States through Ellis Island. Many of them were from Europe.

What was it like for the people who went through Ellis Island? Let's imagine that you were one of them:

The Voyage

Like most of the people who arrive at Ellis Island, you have left your home because you think you can make a better life for yourself in the United States. If you are a man, you might have left your family behind. Men often came first and found jobs and housing. They sent for their families once they were settled.

It takes two weeks to cross the Atlantic Ocean on a steamship. You travel with as many as 2,000 other immigrants. Most immigrants spend most of the voyage below the decks in a part of the ship called the steerage. It is crowded and hard to keep clean. The air is thick with the smells of seasickness and rotten food.

You are excited when you finally see the Statue of Liberty, and you are relieved to know that the voyage is almost over. You are not allowed to enter the United States right away, however. As soon as you get off the steamship, you must board a ferry that takes you to Ellis Island.

Arrival at Ellis Island

Thousands of other immigrants pour into the main building with you. Your ears are filled with the different languages they speak. The immigration officials speak English. You do not understand what they are saying. They point at you and use hand motions to tell you which way to go. You join a long line of people.

It seems to take hours for you to move up in the line. Doctors watch the people in line closely to see if anyone seems sick. They spend only a few seconds with each person, but they must check for sixty different signs of good health.

People who seem sick are examined further. Those with minor illnesses might go to Ellis Island Hospital until they recover. But others with more serious or incurable diseases will be sent back to the country that they came from.

Luckily, you are strong and healthy. You make your way through a maze of passages and railings. Finally, you arrive at the tall desks of the legal inspectors.

Here you are asked many questions. Inspectors ask your name, your age, and where you plan to go. An interpreter translates the inspector's questions into the language you speak, and then translates your answers into English. Children traveling without an adult

Go On

Name ____

must have a letter, telegram, or ticket to show that a relative is waiting for them. During the questioning, some immigrants' names are misspelled. Some are shortened or changed to make them easier to pronounce.

A New Home

After the inspection, you go down some stairs. Immigrants who are going west head for the railroad ticket office. You make your way to the spot where immigrants are reunited with their relatives who have already come to the United States. You find your relatives waiting for you with big smiles and hugs. They will take you to your new home in New York City. There, the streets will be noisy, and your apartment will be crowded with family members. You will have to learn a new language and new customs. Your life will not be easy, but you don't mind. You are ready to start your new life in your new home!

20 Here is a web about Ellis Island. Complete the web with a detail about Ellis Island from the article.

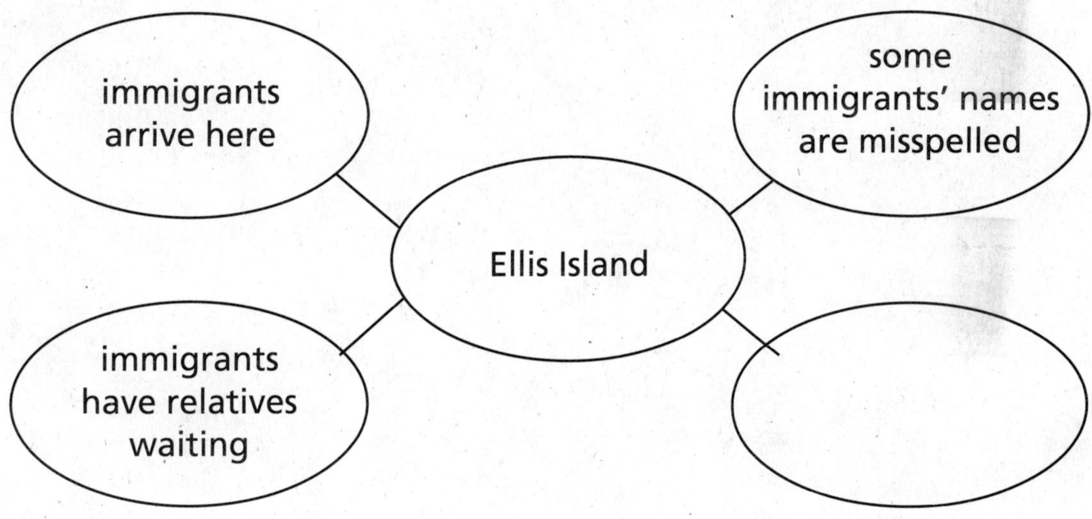

Go On

Name ______________________________

Planning Page

You may PLAN your writing for question 21 here if you wish, but do NOT write your final answer on this page. Your writing on this Planning Page will NOT count toward your final score. Write your final answer beginning on the next page.

Name ______________________________

21

Imagine that it is 100 years ago, and you have left your home in Brazil to come to the United States. Write an article for a newspaper in Brazil describing your trip to America through Ellis Island. Then explain how life in the United States is different from life in Brazil.

In your article, be sure to include

- a title for your article
- a clear beginning, middle, and end to your article
- specific details about Ellis Island and life in the United States

Check your writing for correct spelling, grammar, capitalization, and punctuation.

Go On

Name

STOP

Name ______________________________

Revise and Edit Practice

Sample

There are some mistakes in this paragraph. Let's correct them together.

The new library opened its doors yesterday? Everyone was happy to saw the building finally completed. There are a special room set aside for Computers. Many people do not have computers. In their homes.

Go On

Name ______________________________

Here is a paragraph a student wrote. There are some mistakes in the paragraph. Some sentences may have more than one mistake, and other sentences may contain no mistakes at all. There are no mistakes in spelling.

Read the paragraph, and find the mistakes. Draw a line through each mistake in the paragraph. Then write the correction above it.

Do you have your own computer. My parents bought one for our family. we take turns using it. My Little brother likes to play games. i can type my class papers and make them look neat. My sister looks up information about famous People in history for her class assignments. My parents keep their banking information on the computer? We all has different reasons for using the computer. It gets used all the time.

STOP

Name ______________________________

UNIT 4 TEST

Reading

Directions

In this part of the test, you are going to do some reading. Then you will answer questions about what you have read.

Name ___________________________________

Directions

Read this story about an art fair. Then answer questions 1 through 8.

The School Art Fair

It all started with a notice in the school paper: *Show your work of art at the art fair!*

"I want everyone to bring in something for the fair," our teacher said. "You can work in pairs if you like."

Art really isn't my thing, I thought. I tried to forget about the assignment.

Soon everyone else was working on a project. Luis was making a piñata. Shawna's mother was helping her sew a quilt. Isaac and I just didn't have any ideas. We thought it might help to go to the library.

Candle making? Flower arranging? Origami? None of these things interested me. We were at the end of the encyclopedia when we finally saw it.

"Hey, what do you think of these pictures?" Isaac asked me. The photographs were by William Wegman. They showed a dog dressed-up in different types of clothing.

"These are cool!" I said.

"Exactly! That's just what everyone will think at the fair!" Isaac decided to be an animal photographer. He had some great ideas, but everything he tried turned into a disaster.

"Do we have time to do something like this?" I asked.

"Sure!" Isaac answered. "We'll just put Samson in your sister's clothes. You get him to sit while I take his picture. Simple!"

Isaac came over the next afternoon. We borrowed a beret and a long scarf from my sister.

"These will look great!" Isaac said.

Samson didn't think so. He shook the hat off his head right away. We had used the sombrero my parents got in Mexico.

"I'll tie a string under his chin. Then he can't shake it off," I said. The hat covered his eyes. My mother told us to leave him alone.

"Why don't you walk around the neighborhood and take some pictures?" she suggested.

Our picture wasn't the most exciting one in the art fair. However, my next story will be called "Don't Try This at Home!"

Go On

Name ______________________________

1 According to the story, the problem faced by the main character is

A finding a partner to work with
B planning and completing an art project
C finding a hat for Samson
D a disagreement with his mother

2 Where did the narrator and his partner find an idea for their project?

F a website
G an encyclopedia
H a "How To Do" book
J a newspaper

3 Samson is **most likely**

A the sister
B a classmate
C a dog
D a visitor from Mexico

4 Here is a web about the art fair.

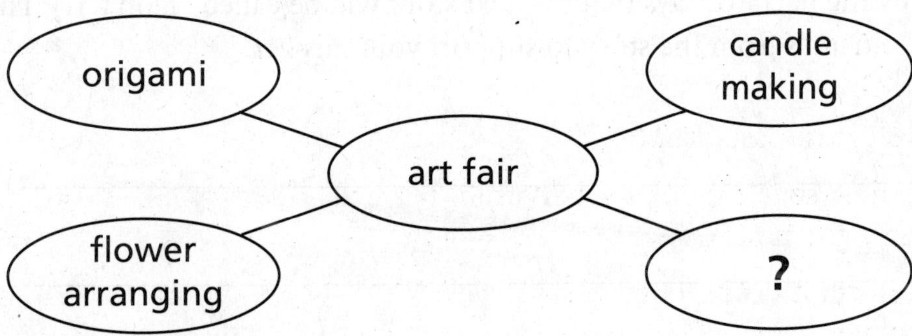

Which phrase **best** completes the web?

F taking pictures
G finding a hat
H going to Mexico
J borrowing a scarf

Go On

Name ______________________________

5 According to the story, a *beret* is

A a hat
B a scarf
C a head
D a string

6 Why did the narrator's mother tell him to leave Samson alone?

F Samson didn't like having his picture taken.
G Samson needed to go for a walk.
H Samson was barking.
J Samson didn't like being dressed up in a hat and scarf.

7 Where did the narrator's mother suggest they take the pictures?

A around the neighborhood
B in the backyard
C at school
D at the library

8 Explain why the narrator says that his next story will be called "Don't Try This at Home!" Use details from the story to support your answer.

____

____

____

____

Name ______________________________

Directions

Read this article about eyes. Then answer questions 9 through 16.

"Eye" Get the Picture

Think about this: Your eye is only about an inch across. But it is the only organ that allows you to sense things at a great distance. If you want to touch or taste something, then that thing must be near you. You can smell something that might not be too close, or hear a sound that might come from even farther away. However, the eye can see light from stars that are millions of miles away.

How does your eye allow you to see? The eye works like a camera. The eye and the camera each have a lens to help make sure that the picture you see is clear.

In the eye, light passes through the pupil, the round hole in the center that looks like a black circle. The iris is the colored part of the eye. Muscles in the iris change the size of the pupil to control the amount of light that enters the eye. A camera has a part that does the same thing. That way your pictures don't come out too light or too dark.

The optic nerve is like the post office. The optic nerve receives the picture from the lens and sends it to the brain. Your brain tells you what you are seeing. The film in the camera works much the same way. Film "sees" and captures the picture from the camera lens.

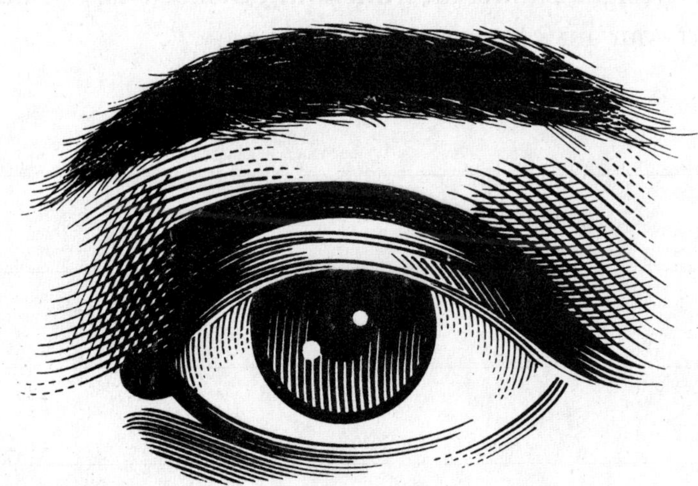

Go On

Name ___

9 According to the passage, a "pupil" is

A the part of the eye that makes the picture clear
B the part of the camera that makes the picture clear
C the part of the eye that light passes through
D the part of the camera that holds the film

10 In this passage, an "iris" is something that

F grows in a garden
G sends messages from the eye to the brain
H makes a picture very clear
J controls the amount of light entering the eye

11 This passage is **mostly** about

A how your eyes and cameras both have lenses
B how your eyes work like a camera
C how your eyes let you see things that are far away
D how your eyes can get tired

12 Explain how your eyesight is different from your other senses. Use details from the passage to support your answer.

___

___

___

___

Name ______________________________

13 The passage compares the optic nerve to a post office

A to show how the eye receives information and sends it to the brain
B to explain why the eye functions smoothly
C to explain why the brain receives clear pictures
D to show how the post office can deliver so many letters

14

The iris __________ too much light from entering the eye.

Choose the word that means the iris prevents too much light from entering the eye.

F allows
G prohibits
H refuses
J permits

15 Which sentence from the passage is an **opinion**?

A The lens makes the picture clear.
B The pupil looks like a black circle.
C The eye is about an inch across.
D The iris is the colored part of the eye.

16 Why did the author **most likely** write this passage?

F to tell a funny story
G to make the reader angry
H to convince the reader to buy eyeglasses
J to give information about the human eye

STOP

Name ____

Listening and Writing

Directions

In this part of the test, you will listen to a story called "Inventions and Inventors." Then you will answer questions about the story.

You will listen to the story twice. The first time you hear the story, listen carefully but do not take notes. As you listen to the story the second time, you may want to take notes. Use the space provided below. You may use these notes to answer the questions that follow. Your notes on this page will NOT count toward your final score.

Notes

Do NOT turn this page until you are told to do so.

Name ______________________________

17 In "Inventions and Inventors," you heard about four important inventions and the people who made them. Describe the inventions made by the people listed. Then explain why you think each invention was important.

Wilbur and Orville Wright

Bill and Mark Richards

Johannes Gutenberg

Tim Berners-Lee

Go On

Name ______________________________

Planning Page

You may PLAN your writing for question 18 here if you wish, but do NOT write your final answer on this page. Your writing on this Planning Page will NOT count toward your final score. Write your final answer beginning on the next page.

Name ______________________________

18

Inventors create something new or improve on something that already exists. Think of an invention you could make. Write a description of your invention. Also explain why your invention is useful and encourage people to try it.

In your description, be sure to include

- a name for your product
- specific details about your invention and why it is important
- convincing language that will make readers want your invention

Check your writing for correct spelling, grammar, capitalization, and punctuation.

STOP

Name ______________________________

Reading and Writing

Directions

In this part of the test, you are going to read a story called "Linda's Library" and an article called "Nellie Bly." You will answer questions 19 through 21 and write about what you have read. You may look back at the story and the article as often as you like.

Name ______________________________

Linda's Library

Linda Green had a huge collection of things to read. The bookshelves in her bedroom were overflowing. One bookshelf was full of silly stories and books of riddles. Another shelf held mysteries featuring young detectives. Her comic books didn't fit on the shelves, so Linda stacked them by her window. She kept her adventure magazines under the bed. Linda was proud of her collection, but she had a problem. When she needed a certain book, it was nearly impossible to find it.

Linda decided to organize her collection. She took the books off the shelves. She took the magazines out from under the bed. She spread all her comic books on the floor. Just then, Linda's mother walked into the room. She did not see Linda. Linda was hidden behind a huge stack of magazines.

"Where are you?" Mrs. Green asked.

"Right here," Linda said. She popped her head up from behind the stack. Mrs. Green looked upset.

"We have a problem," she said.

"I know," Linda said. "I need to organize this mess! I really need more bookshelves."

"There's no room in here for any more books," Mrs. Green said. "In fact, Linda, I think it's time for you to get rid of some of these books. Maybe you can give some of them away to your friends."

"I can't give them away!" Linda cried. "These are my favorites."

"Well, you can't keep all of this stuff in your room. You need to figure out something to get your collection down to a reasonable size," Mrs. Green said.

"Okay, I'll think about it," Linda said. Linda didn't know what to do. She didn't want to give away any of her books, but she knew her mother was right. Her collection was so big it no longer fit in her bedroom, but there was nowhere else in their small apartment to keep it.

The next day at lunch, Linda asked her friends for ideas. "I know!" said Andrea. "You could sell your comic books and make some money."

"I've got it," said Paul. "You can add a room to your apartment!"

Linda shook her head. "I don't want to sell my comic books, and you can't just add a room to an apartment." They were all silent.

Go On

Name ______________________________

"Well, I'm out of ideas," said Paul.

"Me, too," said Andrea. "Let's meet outside the library after school. We might have more ideas by then." The friends waved good-bye and headed back to their classrooms.

Suddenly, Linda smiled. "That's it!" she thought. "The library! That's my solution!"

Linda ran up to Andrea and Paul when she saw them outside the library after school. "I've figured out what to do with my collection," she said. "I'm going to start my own book club."

"What do you mean?" asked Paul.

"It will work like a library. Kids can borrow my books, magazines, and comics for free," Linda explained. "They just have to return them in two weeks."

"But how will that solve your problem?" Andrea asked.

"If enough people borrow my books each week, then I will always have enough room!"

The book club took a lot of planning. Linda's family and friends helped her. There was a job for everyone. First, they organized Linda's collection into categories. Next they made a list of every book, magazine, and comic book she owned. Then they made labels to go inside all of the books. Linda's classroom teacher said she could spend a few minutes before class lending books.

On the first day, Linda's classmates lined up eagerly. "Hey, Linda," called Jack. "Do you have the latest issue of *Adventure* magazine?"

"Yes I do," she said.

"I can't believe I get to read all this cool stuff for free," Jack said. "Great idea!"

"Thanks!" said Linda. The other students were talking excitedly about the books, too. Linda smiled. She was proud that her book club was off to a good start.

Name ____

19 In "Linda's Library," Linda Green has a problem. In the chart below, explain her problem and the three possible solutions she and her friends considered.

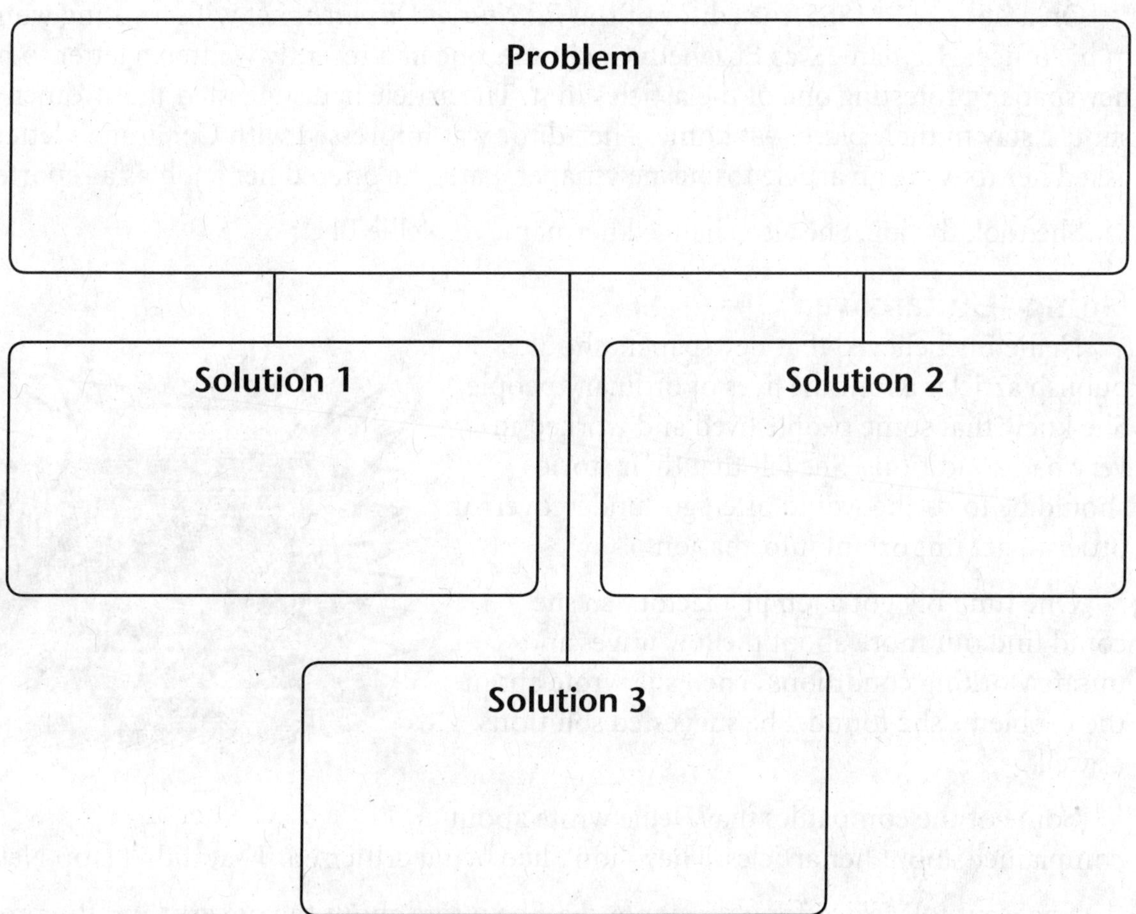

Briefly explain the solution Linda chose and why it was her best choice.

____

____

____

____

____

Go On

Name ______________________________

Nellie Bly

A Reporter is Born

On a hot day in 1855, the editor of the *Pittsburgh Dispatch* met with a young woman in his office. Her name was Elizabeth Cochrane. She had recently written a letter to his newspaper, protesting one of the articles in it. The article had suggested that women should stay in their place—at home. The editor was impressed with Cochrane's letter. He asked her to write an article for his newspaper. Later, he offered her a job as a reporter.

She took the job. She also changed her name to Nellie Bly.

Going "Undercover"

Nellie Bly believed that newspapers should publish articles about the lives of ordinary people. She knew that some people lived and worked in very bad conditions. She felt that their stories should be told. She would often go "undercover" in order to get important information.

One time Bly got a job in a factory so she could find out more about the low wages and unsafe working conditions. Then she wrote about the problems she found. She suggested solutions as well.

Some of the companies that Nellie wrote about complained about her articles. They didn't like being criticized. That didn't stop Nellie Bly.

She went to Mexico for several months. She wrote about the poverty and the problems in the government that she found there. The Mexican government didn't like what she wrote and made her leave the country.

Bly then moved to New York and took a job at a newspaper called the *New York World.* She continued to go undercover to write about poverty, injustice, and other social problems.

One series of articles she wrote was about Blackwell's Island, a home for mentally ill people. Bly pretended to be mentally ill so she would be sent to Blackwell's Island. While she was there, she discovered the terrible conditions in which the patients lived. Her articles about the home helped bring about changes in how the patients were treated.

Nellie Bly also wrote about factories, jails, and the government. She became the best-known woman journalist of her time.

Around the World with Nellie Bly

Nellie Bly often wrote about social problems, but her most famous story was about a trip around the world. In the 1870s, French writer Jules Verne wrote a book called *Around*

Name ______________________________

the World in Eighty Days. This fictional story told about a man who bet that he could travel around the world in eighty days. An editor at the *New York World* wanted to see if a person could really do such a thing. He asked Nellie Bly to try.

Every day, the newspaper published Bly's reports on what she saw and did on her trip. The paper also held a contest to see who could come the closest to guessing how long it would take her to go around the world. Close to one million people entered that contest!

In her travels, Bly rode burros, horses, and trains. She sailed on small boats and large ships. She had many adventures, including one that involved a pet monkey that she took with her. On the Pacific Ocean, her ship crossed into bad weather. Some of the sailors believed that the monkey was causing the storms. They wanted to throw it overboard! Bly persuaded the sailors that the monkey was not responsible for the storms.

When Nellie Bly arrived back in New York, she was greeted by cheering fans. She had beaten Jules Verne's storybook hero! His journey took 80 days, but hers took only 72 days, 6 hours, 11 minutes, and 14 seconds. Her book about her trip, *Around the World in Seventy-two Days,* became very popular.

A Role Model for Reporters

Nellie Bly had an adventurous spirit. She also had great concern for ordinary people. She cared about women, workers, and people who were unable to speak up for themselves. Her courage and caring still inspire reporters today.

Go On

Name ______________________________

20 Nellie Bly often went “undercover” to get information. Describe some of the conditions she wrote about. Use details from the story to support your answer.

Name ______________________________

Planning Page

You may PLAN your writing for question 21 here if you wish, but do NOT write your final answer on this page. Your writing on this Planning Page will NOT count toward your final score. Write your final answer beginning on the next page.

Name ______________________________

21

Books were very important to Nellie Bly and Linda Green. Nellie wrote many articles and a book about her trip around the world. Linda loved reading books. Write a review for the school newspaper about your favorite book.

In your review, be sure to include

- a title for your article
- a description of the book
- why it is your favorite
- a clear beginning, middle, and end to your article

Check your writing for correct spelling, grammar, capitalization, and punctuation.

Name

STOP

Name ______________________________

Revise and Edit Practice

Sample

There are some mistakes in this paragraph. Let's correct them together.

Our class trip will be in November this year. We are going to albany, New York. The state capital are there. The building was built between 1867 and 1899, The city is located on the hudson River.

Go On

Name ______________________________

Here is a paragraph a student wrote. There are some mistakes in the paragraph. Some sentences may have more than one mistake, and other sentences may contain no mistakes at all. There are no mistakes in spelling.

Read the paragraph and find the mistakes. Draw a line through each mistake in the paragraph. Then write the correction above it.

A new restaurant am opening in our neighborhood. The ribbon-cutting ceremony is at noon today. My family want to eat there this weekend. Now we won't have to go all the way downtown. To eat. The restaurant will have nothing but sandwiches for lunch. They will also serve breakfast and dinner every day but sunday. We has waited a long time to get a restaurant in this area.

STOP

Name ______________________________

UNIT 5 TEST

Reading

Directions

In this part of the test you are going to do some reading. Then you will answer questions about what you read.

Name ______________________________

Directions

Read this story about Wanda. Then answer questions 1 through 8.

Wanda's Wasteful Ways

My name is Wanda. I throw away newspaper and junk mail and soft drink cans. I don't recycle them.

TIP As you read the story, think about the meaning of it. Wanda is telling you about her wasteful habits for a reason. Ask yourself, why is Wanda telling me this?

I write notes to myself on lots of sheets of paper. I often throw the notes away without even looking at them.

I waste food, too. I heap my plate high with several servings and then throw most of it in the trash. When we go out to a restaurant, I order a lot even if I'm not very hungry. Sometimes when I ask for ketchup, I simply toss the unused packets instead of returning them.

At home, I turn on the television and the stereo and all the lights. When I leave the room, I do not turn anything off.

When I go outside, I leave the door open even though my mom says we can't afford to heat the whole world.

Then there is all that cold water that runs while I brush my teeth. When I take a bath, I fill the tub to the very top. My great big bath not only wastes water, it also wastes the energy that heated the water.

I know that all these wasteful ways do not help my neighbors. They need food and water, too. Also, all that extra garbage takes up too much space.

I need some help. Maybe you can remind me about what to do. Even better, maybe you can set a good example!

Go On

Name ____________________

1 What is this story **mostly** about?

A How Wanda wastes things
B Where Wanda's mom works
C What Wanda's neighbors do
D When the trash is collected

2 According to the story, how is taking a big bath wasteful?

TIP Think about what the story says about Wanda's big baths. Reread the section if you're unsure of the answer.

F People waste time taking baths.
G Taking a big bath means that extra soap is needed.
H Big baths use more water and energy than necessary.
J Using too much water makes more garbage.

3 Wanda's mom tells her "we can't afford to heat the whole world." What is Wanda's mom telling her to do?

A Turn up the heat
B Close the door
C Come inside
D Pay the heating bill

4 Here is a web about Wanda's wasteful ways.

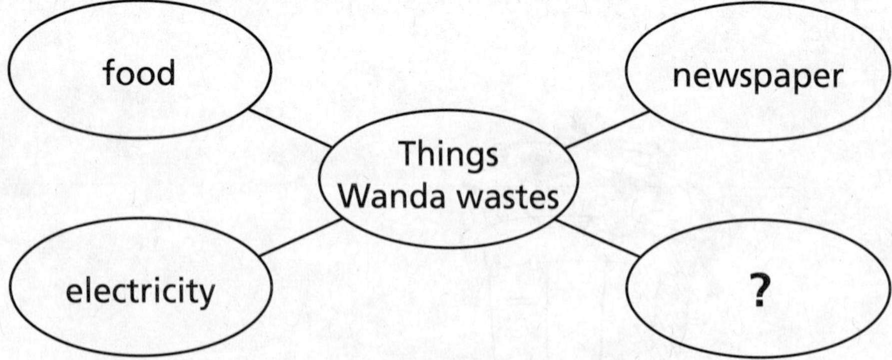

Which word **best** completes the web?

F space
G toothbrush
H neighbors
J water

Name ____

5 Which of these statements **best** summarizes this story?

A Don't waste water.
B Wasteful ways are not good for anyone.
C Throw things away.
D Let the cold water run when you brush your teeth.

TIP Remember that the summary should tell the main idea and important points in one sentence.

6 According to the story, what is one way to set a good example for Wanda?

F Leave the water running while you brush your teeth.
G Throw away newspapers and soft drink cans.
H Turn on lights when you leave a room.
J Turn off the water while you brush your teeth.

7 According to the story, "recycle" means

A throw away
B hide
C put them in the basement
D use again

8 Explain how Wanda's wasteful ways could affect both her family and her neighbors. Use details from the story and your own knowledge to support your answer.

____

____

____

____

Go On

Name ______________________________

Directions

Read this article about an oil spill. Then answer questions 9 through 16.

Pitching In

In 1989, a supertanker was shipwrecked off the coast of Alaska. The giant ship was filled with fuel from Alaska's oilfields. The crash opened a hole in the ship and more than 10 million gallons of heavy black oil spilled into the waters of Prince William Sound. It was the worst oil spill in the history of the United States.

TIP When you're taking a timed test, every minute counts. Look at the questions first, so you'll know what to look for in the passage.

The area was mostly wilderness, but millions of animals lived there. As soon as the people who lived in the area heard about the spill, they rushed to help. The fishers took their boats into Prince William sound to try to collect some of the spilled oil. Other people helped by cleaning the beaches and catching and cleaning the oil-soaked animals.

It took three years to clean up most of the oil. The United States Coast Guard, the state of Alaska, and the oil company itself all pitched in to help. More than 11,000 people worked on the project. The cleanup cost more than two billion dollars. Now we have better ways of building ships to help protect our shores against more oil spills.

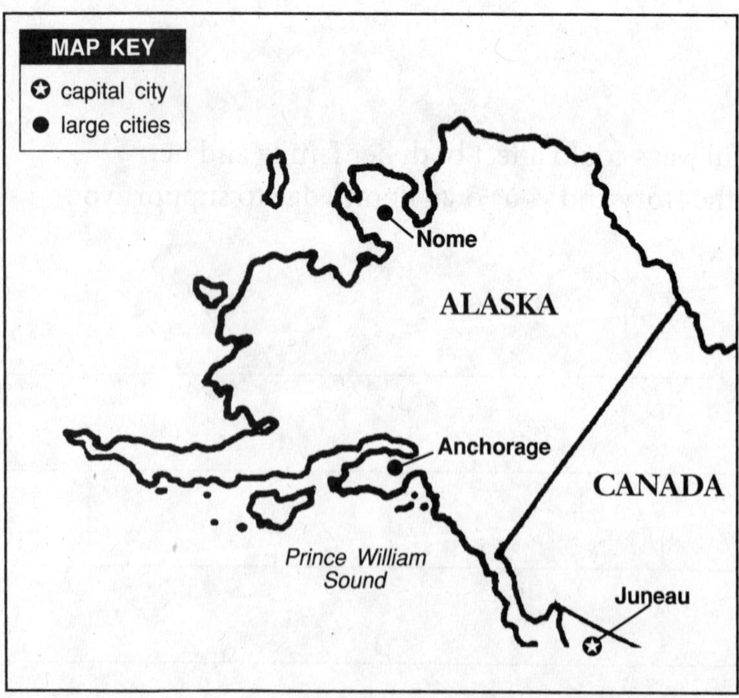

TIP Find Prince William Sound on the map. You will probably have to use the map to answer at least one question.

Name ______________________________

9 According to the article, the word "supertanker" **most likely** means

A heavy oil
B terrible accident
C oilfields
D giant ship

> **TIP** Supertanker is not defined in the article. Use the context of the word in the article and what you already know to figure out what the word means.

10 Which of these statements **best** summarizes this article?

F A ship prevented an accident that would have hurt animals and birds.
G A shipwreck caused a huge oil spill that cost billions of dollars to clean up.
H People worked together to clean the beaches.
J Tankers often sail in Prince William Sound.

11 Study the map. Which city is closest to Prince William Sound?

A Anchorage
B Juneau
C Nome
D Alaska

12 According to the article, the word "Sound" **most likely** means

F noise
G body of water
H long river
J healthy

13 What is the best way to find the answer to Number 10?

A Look at the map.
B Scan the passage.
C Read the title.
D Look for important dates in the passage.

Go On

Name ______________________________

14 According to the article, what is the correct order of these three story events?

1. People rushed to help clean up.

2. A ship crashed near Alaska.

3. Black oil spilled into the water.

F 1, 2, 3
G 2, 3, 1
H 2, 1, 3
J 3, 2, 1

15 According to the article, the 1989 crash was the worst in

A Alaska's history
B United States history
C world history
D twenty years

16 Explain what the title of the article means. Use details from the article to support your answer.

____

____

____

STOP

Name ______________________________

Listening and Writing

Directions

In this part of the test, you are going to listen to a story called "The Unstoppable Clara Barton." Then you will answer questions about the story.

You will listen to the story twice. The first time you hear the story, listen carefully but do not take notes. As you listen to the story for the second time, you may want to take notes. Use the space provided below. You may use these notes to answer the questions that follow. Your notes on this page will NOT count toward your final score.

Notes

Do NOT turn this page until you are told to do so.

Name ______________________________

17 The article talks about several ways Clara Barton helped others during her life. Describe three ways she helped people and, for each way, explain who may have been helped.

The first way she helped people was

____

This helped . . .

____

The second way she helped people was

____

This helped . . .

____

The third way she helped people was

____

This helped . . .

____

Name ______________________________

Planning Page

You may PLAN your writing for question 18 here if you wish, but do NOT write your final answer on this page. Your writing on this Planning Page will NOT count toward your final score. Write your final answer beginning on the next page.

Name ______________________________

18

Suppose you had had an opportunity to meet Clara Barton. Write a personal letter to her, explaining how you feel about her work. Use information from "The Unstoppable Clara Barton" to write your letter.

In your letter, be sure to include

- a greeting, body, and closing
- specific details from "The Unstoppable Clara Barton"
- your personal feelings about her work

Check your writing for correct spelling, grammar, capitalization, and punctuation.

STOP

Name

Reading and Writing

Directions

In this part of the test, you are going to read a story called "Bringing the Elms Back to Elm Street" and an article called "Tell the World." You will answer questions 19 through 21 and write about what you have read. You may look back at the story and the article as often as you like.

Go On

Name ____

Bringing the Elms Back to Elm Street

Steven lives on Birch Street. His backyard has two tall birch trees, and there are three more birch trees on the street in front of his house. Squirrels and chipmunks run up the thin white trunks. Birds build nests in the bushy branches.

Steven's grandmother lives on Elm Street. One day Steven visited his grandmother. He noticed that there were no elm trees on Elm Street. He decided to ask her why.

"Grandma," he said, "I live on Birch Street, where a lot of birch trees grow. Why is your street called Elm Street? I've never seen an elm tree here."

"There were elm trees once, Steven," said his grandmother, "but they were gone long before you were born. In 1942, when I was a little girl, Dutch elm disease started making the trees sick."

"What's Dutch elm disease?" asked Steven.

"Dutch elm disease wilts the elm trees' leaves and causes them to fall off. Then the disease spreads to the rest of the tree and kills it."

"That's too bad," said Steven. "What were the elm trees like?"

"They were just beautiful," said his grandmother. "Some were 100 feet tall! Their big, leafy branches formed a canopy that covered the entire street. Walking down the street was like walking under an umbrella."

"There must have been a lot of trees to give that much shade," said Steven.

"Oh yes. The trees grew from one end of the street to the other," said his grandmother. "There was a tall elm in my backyard with a tire swing. I used to have so much fun swinging on it. Then the elm trees slowly began to die. Before long, the whole street was bare. I missed the trees very much. I still do."

When Steven went home, he thought about what his grandmother had said. He wished that she could enjoy trees in her backyard as he did. He began to wonder if there was a cure for the disease that made the elm trees sick. He decided to find out.

Steven researched elm trees on the Internet and learned some good news. Government scientists had been working for more than twenty years to develop elm trees that could not get Dutch elm disease. Two such trees, the Valley Forge and New Harmony elms, were now available.

"That's great!" Steven thought. "Grandma's birthday is next week. Maybe I could surprise her with an elm tree."

Name ____

The next day Steven went with his mother to a plant store. He spoke with one of the clerks who worked there. She told him more about the new elms.

"These new trees have been tested over and over," the clerk explained. "Like the old trees, these trees grow quickly. They are able to survive cold winters, too."

The clerk helped Steven choose two healthy Valley Forge saplings. Both young trees were about four feet tall. They looked like thin tree branches, but the clerk explained that when they were planted, leaves would appear. She told Steven how to dig holes to plant the trees. She explained how to care for the trees as they grew.

Steven couldn't wait to give his grandmother her gift. On her birthday, he took the saplings to her.

"Where on earth did you find these?" she asked.

Then Steven told her about the new kinds of elms and how he found out about them.

"Thank you so much for this wonderful present, Steven," she said. "You have brought the elms back to Elm Street!"

Go On

Name ______________________________

19 Here is a chart about Dutch elm disease. Complete the chart with an event that happens last.

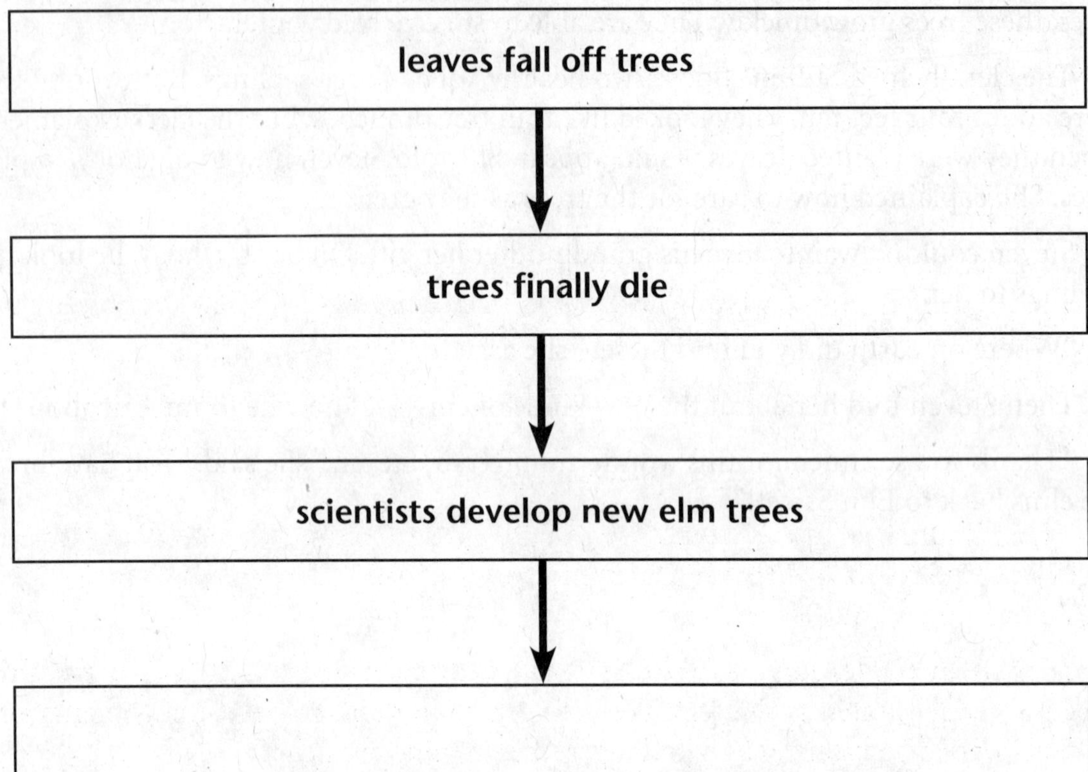
leaves fall off trees
trees finally die
scientists develop new elm trees

Name ______________________________

Tell the World

Communities are made up of many people. Each person shares a responsibility for that community. What can a person do if he or she finds something that needs to be changed in the local community or the world?

Severn Suzuki was a 12-year-old girl who lived in Vancouver, Canada. Severn had always enjoyed nature. She loved going camping and fishing. One day she went fishing with her dad and learned that the fish were full of cancers.

Severn began to worry about the environment. She worried about plants and animals. She worried about the children who were going hungry. Severn knew she had to do something.

She became a member of the Environmental Children's Organization (ECO). This group of 12- and 13-year-olds from Canada wanted to stop the destruction of the world. Group members wanted to keep the world safe for future generations.

The group raised money to travel 6,000 miles (9,654 kilometers) to the Earth Summit in Rio de Janeiro, Brazil. Members planned to speak before the United Nations Conference on Environment and Development.

More than 100 leaders and members of environmental organizations were at this meeting. They wanted to figure out how to save plants and animals. Many plants and animals were disappearing and in danger of becoming extinct.

Severn Suzuki was one of the four children who spoke at the conference. In her speech, she shared her biggest fears:

> "Losing my future is not like losing an election or a few points on the stock market. I am here to speak for all generations to come.
>
> I am here to speak on behalf of the starving children around the world whose cries go unheard.
>
> I am here to speak for the countless animals dying across this planet because they have nowhere left to go. We cannot afford to be unheard.
>
> I am afraid to go out in the sun now because of the holes in the ozone. I am afraid to breathe the air because I don't know what chemicals are in it.
>
> I used to go fishing in Vancouver with my dad until just a few years ago we found the fish full of cancers. And now we hear about animals and plants going extinct every day—vanishing forever.
>
> In my life, I have dreamt of seeing the great herds of wild animals, jungles and rain forests full of birds and butterflies, but now I wonder if they will even exist for my children to see.

Go On

Name ______________________________

Did you have to worry about these little things when you were my age?

All this is happening before our eyes, and yet we act as if we have all the time we want and all the solutions.

I'm only a child and I don't have all the solutions, but I want you to realize neither do you!"

She begged the leaders, "If you don't know how to fix it, please stop breaking it!" Severn reminded them, "We are all in this together and should act as one single world working toward one single goal."

Many people were moved by Severn Suzuki's speech. She told the world exactly how she felt. That was the first step to making a difference.

20 Explain what the title of the article means. Use details from the article to support your answer.

____

____

____

____

Name ______________________________

Planning Page

You may PLAN your writing for question 21 here if you wish, but do NOT write your final answer on this page. Your writing on this Planning Page will NOT count toward your final score. Write your final answer beginning on the next page.

Name ______________________________

21

Steven and Severn both worked to solve problems with the environment. Write a speech that you could present to the students in your school. In your speech, talk about ways you and your classmates could help solve a problem in the world.

In your speech, be sure to
- describe the problem you want to solve
- explain why the issue is a problem
- support your opinions with facts
- urge your classmates to help you solve the problem

Check your writing for correct spelling, grammar, capitalization, and punctuation.

Name

STOP

Name ______________________________

Revise and Edit Practice

Sample

There are some mistakes in this paragraph. Let's correct them together.

The Eastern Bluebird is the state bird of New York. the male bird has bright blue feathers and a white Belly. The female bird has dull blue wings and tail and a white belly. These songbirds has a melodic warble. The birds mostly eats insects and worms. It also eat fruit.

Name ______________________________

Here is a paragraph a student wrote. There are some mistakes in the paragraph. Some sentences may have more than one mistake, and other sentences may contain no mistakes at all. There are <u>no</u> mistakes in spelling.

Read the paragraph and find the mistakes. Draw a line through each mistake in the paragraph. Then write the correction above it.

What animals do you like. I like cats. I like big cats and small cats. I have a Bombay cat. Her name is Sleek. Her fur is black and look shiny like patent leather. She likes to be brushed. She resembles a small panther. sleek likes a lot of attention. She follow me from room to room. I does not let her go outside. She's glad to see me when i get home from school.

STOP

Name ______________________________

UNIT 6 TEST

Reading

Directions

In this part of the test, you are going to do some reading. Then you will answer questions about what you have read.

Name ______________________________

Directions

Read this folktale about a reed pipe. Then answer questions 1 through 7.

The Golden Reed Pipe (A Folktale from China)

Long ago in China, there lived a woman and her daughter. The daughter was called Little Red because she loved red clothing. One day, a dragon swooped down and carried Little Red away. Her mother heard Little Red's voice crying:

Oh mother, oh mother, as dear as can be,
My brother, my brother will rescue me!

The poor mother did not know what to think, as she had no son. Then one day she found a lost little boy under a bright red berry plant. She named him Redberry.

Redberry was outside when he heard a crow cry:

You have a sister out there, out there!
Save her from the dragon's lair!

Redberry ran to his mother, who told him about Little Red and what had happened. So the boy set out to rescue his sister. He walked until he came to a large rock. He rolled the rock away and found a shiny golden reed pipe.

When Redberry blew on the pipe, all the frogs and other creatures began to dance. The faster he played the tune, the faster they danced.

"Aha!" cried Redberry. "Now I can deal with the dragon!"

When he came to the dragon's cave, he saw a girl dressed in red. Redberry blew on the pipe, and the dragon began to dance. The faster Redberry played, the faster the dragon danced. At last the dragon cried:

I'll send her home
If you leave me alone!

Redberry knew better than to believe a dragon. He kept on playing until they came to the sea. With a splash, the dragon fell in! Then the sister and brother returned home to their mother, who smiled with joy to see them.

Go On

Name ____

1 This story **most likely**

A is based on real events
B was first told long ago
C was made up and written down by a person in Japan
D was written to give facts about a musical instrument

2 According to the folktale, the mother named the boy Redberry because

F he liked to eat berries
G he wanted to find his sister
H she found him under a red bush
J she liked red plants

3 According to the folktale, which of these events happens **first**?

A Little Red's mother finds Redberry.
B Little Red says her brother will rescue her.
C Redberry moves the rock.
D Redberry sees the dragon.

4 Here is a web about this folktale.

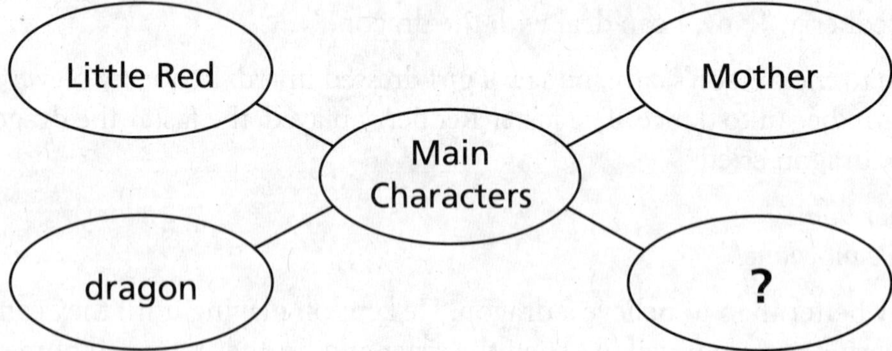

Which word **best** completes the web?

F Golden
G rock
H Redberry
J music

Name ______________________________

5 When Redberry sees the frogs and other creatures dancing, he gets the idea

- **A** to keep the animals as pets
- **B** to entertain the dragon with his music
- **C** to make his living playing the golden reed pipe
- **D** to make the dragon dance and not let him stop

6 According to the folktale, why did Redberry keep playing after the dragon said he would send Little Red home?

- **F** Redberry didn't want Little Red to come home.
- **G** Redberry didn't trust the dragon.
- **H** Redberry liked playing the golden reed pipe.
- **J** Redberry wanted to go swimming in the sea.

7 Explain how Redberry knew what to do with the reed pipe. Use details from the folktale to support your answer.

____

____

____

____

Go On

Name ____________________

Directions

Read this article. Then answer questions 8 through 15.

The Overland Mail System

In the early 1800s, there wasn't a great need for fast mail service and safe passage to the West. Only two steamships carried mail and passengers from the east coast to the west coast each month. The ships had to go all the way around South America, and the journey easily would take more than a month. In addition to being slow, steamship travel could be dangerous because of violent storms. Passengers often became seasick. Some people caught tropical diseases, which made the long journey even worse. The California gold rush and westward expansion created a demand for fast, safe mail and passenger service from coast to coast.

In order to meet this new need, the Overland Mail Route was created. The first Overland Mail run began in St. Louis, Missouri, on September 16, 1858. Passengers and mail began the journey by train. Where the railroad stopped, they continued by stagecoach. They arrived at Fort Smith, a military outpost in Arkansas, on September 19.

From Fort Smith, the Overland Mail Route went across the frontier to what is now El Paso, Texas. It continued on to Tucson and Los Angeles. Its final stop was San Francisco. The soldiers who lived at Fort Smith helped early pioneers and gold miners make the long and dangerous journey west. The entire trip took just under twenty-four days.

The Overland Mail system was made up of a network of collection boxes and stations not unlike the system we use today. Men called "mail riders" would pick up mail near a stagecoach station. In some places, mail was left for the mail rider at an agreed-on fence or gatepost. Mail riders took the mail they picked up to farms that were used as collection stations. The farmers were stationmasters. Their wives sold food to the passengers and stagecoach drivers who stopped to pick up the mail.

There were 141 original stations on the 2,795-mile trail between St. Louis, Missouri, and San Francisco, California. The number of stations soon grew to 200 as hotels and other businesses were built along the route.

Name ______________________________

8 Which statement from the article is an **opinion**?

A Gold was discovered in California in 1848.
B There were 141 original Overland Mail stations.
C Fort Smith was the best stop on the Overland Mail Route.
D San Francisco was the final stop on the Overland Mail Route.

9 Why was the Overland Mail Route created?

F People moving west needed faster mail service.
G Steamships couldn't carry both mail and passengers.
H Steamships stopped sailing to the west coast.
J More goods had to be transported to the West.

10 Which statement from the article is a **fact**?

A Farmers didn't make very good stationmasters.
B The Overland Mail Route to California was better than the sea route.
C The Overland Mail Route began in Missouri and ended in California.
D The farmers' wives sold delicious food.

11 Explain what the journey by ship from the east coast to the west coast was like. Use details from the article to support your answer.

____

____

____

____

Go On

Name ______________________________

12 Here is a web about the stations on the Overland Mail System.

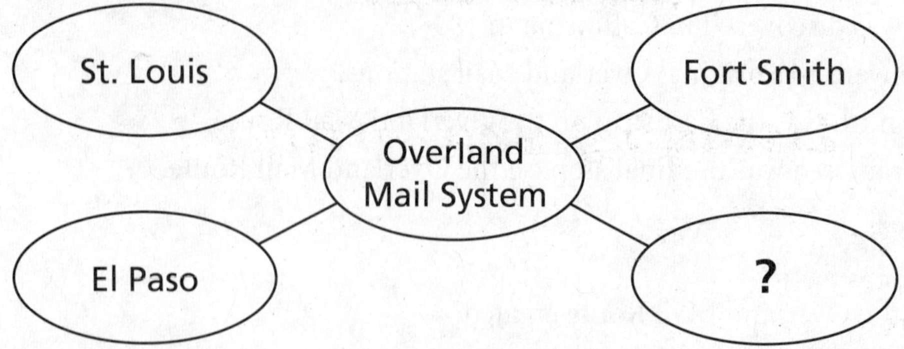

Which station name **best** completes the web?

F Albany
G Orlando
H Chicago
J San Francisco

13 Why did the author **most likely** write this passage?

A to give information about a mail service
B to make readers laugh
C to tell a story about a horse
D to convince the reader to ride a stagecoach

14 How long did the first trip on the Overland Mail Route take?

F 3 days
G 2 weeks
H 24 days
J more than a month

15 According to the article, why was the Overland Mail Route important?

A It connected the eastern and western parts of the country.
B It helped farmers make money.
C It started the California gold rush.
D It connected military outposts.

STOP

Name ______________________________

Listening and Writing

Directions

In this part of the test, you are going to listen to a story called "Cooking in the 1700s and 1800s." Then you will answer questions about the story.

You will listen to the story twice. The first time you hear the story, listen carefully but do not take notes. As you listen to the story for the second time, you may want to take notes. Use the space provided below. You may use these notes to answer the questions that follow. Your notes on this page will NOT count toward your final score.

Notes

Do NOT turn this page until you are told to do so.

Name ______________________________

16 Cooking in the 1700s and 1800s was a major chore. Compare and contrast colonial and pioneer cooking by completing the following chart.

	Colonial Cooking in the 1700s	Pioneer Cooking in the 1800s
Kitchens	Colonial kitchens were often separate from the house.	
Appliances		Pioneers did not have a stove, a refrigerator, running water, or electricity.
Servants	Wealthy colonists usually had servants to cook for them.	
Preserving Foods		Pioneers had to preserve foods to make them last.

Name ____________________

Planning Page

You may PLAN your writing for question 17 here if you wish, but do NOT write your final answer on this page. Your writing on this Planning Page will NOT count toward your final score. Write your final answer beginning on the next page.

Name ______________________________

17 Would you rather be a colonist in the 1700s or a pioneer in the early 1800s? Choose one, and write an essay about what your life is like as a colonist or a pioneer. Be sure to explain your choice and use information from the passage to describe your life.

Check your writing for correct spelling, grammar, capitalization, and punctuation.

STOP

Name ______________________________

Reading and Writing

Directions

In this part of the test, you will read a story called "A Piece of the Past" and an article called "The Many Forms of Money." You will answer questions 18 through 20 and write about what you have read. You may look back at the story and the article as often as you like.

Go On

Name ____________________

A Piece of the Past

Nate sat on a pile of dirt in the backyard. It was a warm spring day. He wiped the sweat off his forehead and ran his fingers through the soil. "The vegetables are going to do well in this dirt," he thought.

A few days ago, Nate's dad had suggested that they start a vegetable garden. Nate's dad knew a lot about plants. He had always wanted to teach Nate about gardening, but their old house didn't have a yard. They had just moved into a new house, and it had a yard with space for a garden. Nate eagerly volunteered to do some of the planting. He liked being out in the sun. He also liked the feel of the damp earth between his fingers. His father bought several small plants to start their garden. This summer, they would grow tomatoes, lettuce, and squash.

Before they started, Nate and his dad drew a map of the garden. They planned where they would plant each vegetable. Nate's dad showed him how to dig a hole in the dirt. He also showed him how to handle each plant. Together, they planted six tomato plants. "In a few weeks, we will have juicy, ripe tomatoes to eat," his dad said.

"Can we use them to make pizza sauce?" Nate asked.

"Sure," his dad said with a laugh. "Now planting the lettuce seeds is the next task. You can do that by yourself. Call me if you need me."

Nate put his hands in the dirt. He used a small garden shovel to turn over the earth. The more he dug, the cooler the dirt became. He picked out a large rock. Then the tool hit something sharp and smooth. Nate carefully dug under the object and then pulled it from the dirt. It was small, black, and shaped like a triangle. Nate rubbed all the dirt off the object. "Hey, Dad!" he called. "I found something!"

"What is it?" his dad called from inside.

"I don't know," Nate said. "You need to come see it." Nate's dad came outside. The sun glinted off the shiny black object. Nate handed it to him.

"Well, look at that," his dad said softly.

"What is it?" Nate asked.

His father held the object up to the sunlight. "It's an arrowhead," he said.

"Really?" asked Nate. "Those were used for hunting animals, right?"

"Yes. Native Americans used bows and arrows to hunt all kinds of animals, including buffalo," his dad explained. "I can't believe you found an arrowhead in our backyard." Nate's family was part Native American, but they lived far away from Montana, where their ancestors had lived.

"Dad, did you ever hunt buffalo?" Nate asked.

Name ___

"No, of course not. The buffalo were gone long before I was born, but our ancestors hunted buffalo long ago."

"How did they hunt buffalo with this small thing?" Nate said, holding up the arrowhead.

As they sat in the garden, Nate's dad explained that the land where their ancestors lived was once covered with buffalo herds. He said that their ancestors had relied on the buffalo for meat and used their skins for warmth. "No part of the buffalo was wasted," he explained. As Nate listened, he imagined the buffalo running in huge herds across the broad plains.

As the sun began to move toward the west, long shadows fell across the yard.

"Hey, Dad!" Nate exclaimed. "There's a buffalo right there!" He squinted into the sunlight. His dad laughed.

"I think you've been out in the sun too long," he said. "That's the neighbor's dog."

"I know," Nate said. "I just wish it were a buffalo."

"Let's go inside," his dad said. "It's been quite a day." They gathered up their tools and Nate brushed the dirt off his clothes. He couldn't wait to show the arrowhead to his friends and tell them what his dad had told him about his ancestors. He knew they would be as excited as he was to actually hold something from the past.

He took one last look at the arrowhead and then put it in his pocket. He and his dad walked inside, both of them thinking about the buffalo and the people of long ago.

Go On

Name ____

18 Nate and his dad were planting a garden when Nate found an arrowhead. Fill in this sequence chart to show what happened in the story.

Title:	
Characters	**Setting**

First:

↓

Next:

↓

Then:

↓

Last:

Name ____________________

The Many Forms of Money

What do dollars, Euros, yen, and rupees have in common? They are all forms of money. Every day, people around the world use money to buy things. But what exactly is money?

Money helps people trade one thing for another. People trade something of value, such as their work, for money. Then they can trade the money for something they want, such as clothes or food.

Coins and paper bills are useful as money because they stand for a certain value. They are also small and easy to carry and exchange. Money is made in amounts that can be divided easily. For example, one United States dollar can be divided into two half-dollars, four quarters, ten dimes, twenty nickels, or 100 pennies.

In the past, money was often made from things people liked and wanted. In different places feathers, cocoa beans, grains, blocks of salt, stones, and shells have been used. North American Indians used wampum—belts, sashes, or strings of beads—as money.

The first metal coins came into use in China about 3,000 years ago. At first, people in China used metal tools such as spades or knives, as money. Later, miniature spades were used. In time, these became round coins with square holes for stringing the coins together.

The first modern coins were made around 2,400 years ago in what is now Turkey. They were made from a mixture of gold and silver. A picture was stamped on each coin to tell how much it was worth. Before this type of stamped coin, people had to weigh lumps of metal each time they bought or sold something. This was a lot of trouble. Having stamped coins made buying and selling easier.

Paper money was invented in China, perhaps as early as the ninth century. The Chinese government printed pieces of paper with different designs. The designs showed what each piece of paper money was worth.

European settlers brought coins and paper money to North America. American colonists used coins from Spain, England, France, and the Netherlands as money. They also used nails, wampum, beaver pelts, and musket balls. Spanish "pieces of eight" were popular. These were large round silver coins that could be cut like a pie into eight wedge-shaped pieces called bits. Two bits equaled one-quarter of the whole. Even today, some people in the United States still use the nickname "two bits" for a quarter.

Today, every country around the world has its own money. Each country's currency has a particular design, worth, and history. For example, the United States uses dollars and cents, Japan uses yen, and India uses rupees.

For centuries, each European country had its own currency. Italy had lira, France had francs, and so on. Each had a different value. In 2002, twelve European countries agreed

Go On

Name ______________________________

to use a single currency called a Euro. Having the same currency makes travel and trade between countries in Europe much easier.

In the United States today, the most common place to store money is a bank. Many people have checking accounts. Writing checks is one way of exchanging money. People write checks or use debit cards to get money out of their checking accounts.

With computers, new forms of money have come into use. In many places, people can buy "smart cards," such as prepaid phone or gas cards. Computers "read" the cards and keep track of amounts used. In Hong Kong, more than ten million people use a smart-card system called "Octopus." People can buy an Octopus card and use it to pay bus and subway fares and parking fees. They can also use it in convenience stores and fast food restaurants. People can add value to the card when it runs out and can get a refund for unused value.

The Internet has also brought new forms of money exchange. People never have to touch coins, checks, cards, or bills. The click of a computer mouse is all it takes to move money from a bank account to pay for something online.

19 Here is a web with the names of money from some countries. Complete the web with another two names of money from the article.

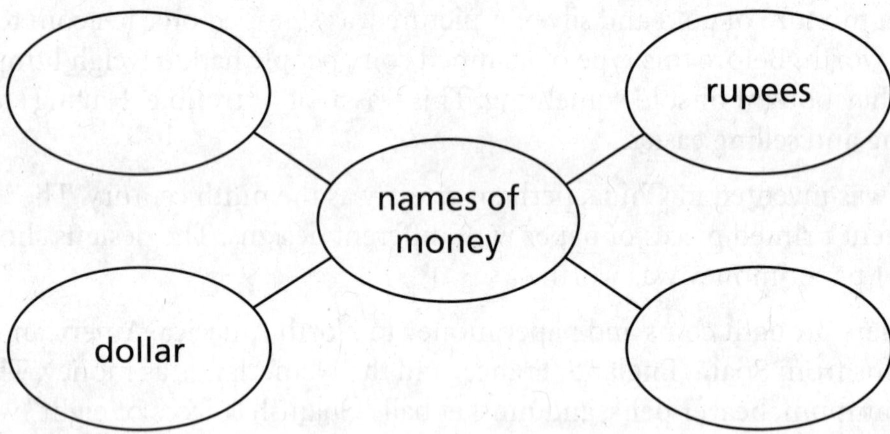

Name ______________________________

Planning Page

You may PLAN your writing for question 20 here if you wish, but do NOT write your final answer on this page. Your writing on this Planning Page will NOT count toward your final score. Write your final answer beginning on the next page.

Name ______________________________

20 Both of these passages talk about ways that we are connected with the past, through early hunting tools and forms of money. Think of a product we use today, such as computers, cell phones, or automobiles. Imagine that someone finds this product hundreds of years from now. What will this product tell future generations about us? Write an essay about <u>one</u> product we use today and what it could tell future generations about us.

Check your writing for correct spelling, grammar, capitalization, and punctuation.

Name

STOP

Name ____

Revise and Edit Practice

Sample

There are some mistakes in this paragraph. Let's correct them together.

I don't like cold weather. the temperature this morning was 38 degrees. That are just a few degrees above freezing? I had a big breakfast with hot oatmeal and toast. I had to put on a heavy coat and heavy boots to go outside. i hope it get warm soon.

Name ______________________________

Here is a paragraph a student wrote. There are some mistakes in the paragraph. Some sentences may have more than one mistake, and other sentences may contain no mistakes at all. There are <u>no</u> mistakes in spelling.

Read the paragraph and find the mistakes. Draw a line through each mistake in the paragraph. Then write the correction above it.

When I awoke this morning, the street was covered with snow. Our yard looking like a winter wonderland. My Brother and I is going to shovel the driveway and the sidewalk. In front of our house. If we finish early, we'll try to help some of our neighbors? That's a good way for us to earn extra money for the Holidays. I can use the money to buy presents for my family.

STOP